SUPER LATE BLOOMER

MY EARLY DAYS IN TRANSITION

AN UP AND OUT COLLECTION

Julia Kaye

Andrews McMeel
PUBLISHING®

before

I didn't always know I was trans.

I mean, I grew up knowing I was different in a way I could never put my finger on, but I didn't know I was *trans*.

I may not have understood myself, but I do remember from a very young age I felt I had to hide myself away. I began trying to change my behavior in an attempt to fit in. The social cues coming from every direction told me that who I was was not okay. I learned that my wants were shameful and, over the years, became secretive about them.

At the onset of puberty, I remember feeling increasingly uncomfortable as my body started becoming masculine. *Surely everyone around me feels the same way,* I thought. It never occurred to me to bring it up to anyone.

The discomfort wasn't something that was constantly on my mind—it stayed in the background, a low-level feeling I simply lived with. Sometimes it would lessen when I became distracted by life, and, when it did, I would think, *maybe I've finally beaten it; maybe I've finally embraced myself as a masculine person and can move on.* But gender dysphoria doesn't work like that. It comes and goes in waves. As I grew older, the discomfort increased.

When I was about twenty-three, I noticed my body changing further: My beard was filling out, my body hair steadily increasing. Testosterone was wreaking havoc on my body and my emotions, exacerbating my dysphoria. Awful memories of early puberty came flooding back. *It's okay,* I told myself countless times. *It's just more to get used to. Everyone feels this way as they get older. You'll get over it in time. Just accept it.*

I had no idea why I felt the way I did, but I became an expert in coping with these feelings through denial.

A year passed before I stumbled onto a website where people documented their transitions while undergoing hormonal replacement therapy. At the time, I vaguely knew that trans people existed in the abstract, but I had never given them much thought before. But now, with images of real trans people bettering their lives right in front of my eyes, I felt an immediate connection: a gut feeling that was so right, like nothing I had ever felt before. *This is a real thing? That real people can do? I want that. Wait . . . I want that?* I didn't understand it, but I became obsessed.

I started reading everything I could find about trans people: about why they transitioned and how it eased their gender dysphoria. But when I thought about how transitioning might apply to me, and everything I'd need to go through to make it happen in my life, I became terrified. So much so that I ended up repressing my feelings and carried on with my life as if nothing had ever happened.

Another year later, I rediscovered the concept and quickly found myself consumed. The thoughts and anxiety surfaced again—distracting me at work, causing me to lose sleep. Round and round I would go in my head: *Could I really be trans? Is this truly what I need? What if I'm not trans enough and it's all a big mistake? Is wanting to be a girl the same as being a girl? This doesn't make any sense. I have a pretty good life; I should just be happy. What would people say? There's no way—this is too out there. I can't tell anyone about this.* Again, I got scared and repressed.

Yet another year passed, and I found myself back in the same place all over again. As much as I might have wanted them to, these thoughts and feelings weren't going away and needed addressing. At twenty-six years old, I finally started to seriously consider the idea of transitioning. I thought about it day and night for months on end. I desperately wanted to make sense of it all, but all I had was my dysphoria and a gut feeling to go off of. It felt like an impossible choice—I'd feel absolutely certain one day and confused the next as my dysphoria came and went. How could I possibly make a decision?

Despite my inner turmoil, it's not as if my everyday life was all doom and gloom. At the time, I was residing in a small farming town in western Massachusetts with my long-term girlfriend, living my childhood dream of drawing comics. We didn't have much, but it was a good life. *I'm happier than I've ever been,* I'd think. *Why isn't it enough?* I wished so much for it to be enough. I was terrified of telling her about my dysphoria. It was the only secret I'd kept to myself over the years.

I tried repeatedly to tell her but felt absolutely paralyzed each time. Everything I learned over the course of my life told me that I shouldn't bring it up; so much so that it felt like I *couldn't* bring it up. But if I was going to figure this out, the most important person in my life needed to know.

One day, in late spring of 2015, while on a walk around the farmland, I somehow mustered up the courage to tell her I was having gender-identity issues that I needed to work through.

She was incredible. Over the next few months, she did everything she could to help me feel more comfortable with myself. She gave me a safe space to experiment with femininity, for which I'll never be able to thank her enough. But, as time went on, it became clear I needed more—it didn't matter how I presented myself; the problem was my body itself.

And so, with extreme trepidation, I told her I needed to transition.

After a few days of packing and a tearful hug good-bye, I was on a flight across the country to move back in with my parents. I started seeing a gender therapist, and, after a few months of intense therapy, I started the process of coming out to my family. I still don't know how I got through those conversations. I doubt anything I ever do in life will be half as difficult as coming out to the people who raised me and the siblings with whom I grew up.

My anxieties about going on hormones (*What if I'm not trans enough and this is all a mistake?*) were overwhelming right until the moment I held the medication in my hand. Almost immediately after taking the pills, I felt a combination of relief and euphoria. The reaction had nothing to do with the pills themselves but instead the knowledge that, despite everything working against this moment, I had finally taken a step toward my new life. It felt good like nothing else I had ever experienced.

For the next few months, I was walking on air, feeling like I had a new lease on life. I was tearing down the self-imposed mental constraints I'd built up over the years and put myself to the task of discovering exactly who I really was.

I began drawing the comics in this book after having been on hormones for four months. Despite being out to my close friends and family, I didn't have any trans people in my life to talk to, which left me feeling isolated. I didn't know how to talk about anything that I was going through in a way that anyone in my life could relate to or understand, so I started pouring my experiences into these comics. I drew a comic nearly every day, making art that documented all my small joys, setbacks, self-directed prejudices, anxieties, and triumphs.

Making these comics helped me navigate the early days of my transition and the complexities of dealing with gender dysphoria. It was a highly personal experience, but, though my story is uniquely mine, I am far from alone. I hope—whether cis, trans, nonbinary, agender, or any other designation on the gender spectrum—you get something out of these comics too.

—Julia

I USED TO BE BETTER

AT IGNORING MY INTERNAL SELF-HATRED

I COULD DISTRACT MYSELF

WITH NEW CLOTHES

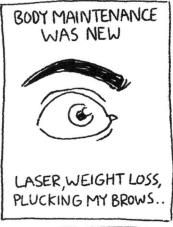

BODY MAINTENANCE WAS NEW

LASER, WEIGHT LOSS, PLUCKING MY BROWS..

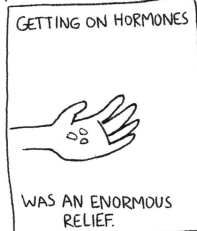

GETTING ON HORMONES

WAS AN ENORMOUS RELIEF.

BUT REALITY HAS

FINALLY SET IN

THERE'S NOTHING LEFT TO DO

BUT WAIT.

MAY 8TH, 2016

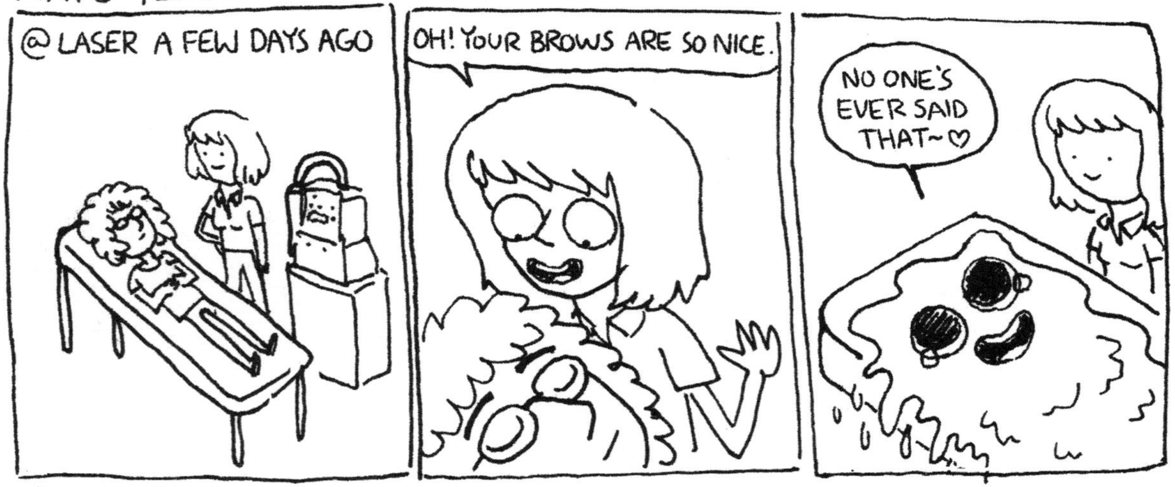
@LASER A FEW DAYS AGO
OH! YOUR BROWS ARE SO NICE.
NO ONE'S EVER SAID THAT~♡

MAY 13TH, 2016

I FELT REALLY GREAT ABOUT MYSELF TODAY!

GROCERY STORE SUSHI

I WISH I COULD BOTTLE THIS FEELING

TO BRIGHTEN UP MY DARKER DAYS.

GOING OUTSIDE IS

TERRIFYING. EXHILARATING

I NOTICE EVERY GLANCE, EVERY STARE THAT SAYS

"YOU'RE DIFFERENT"

A CAR FULL OF MEN SHOUTED AT ME.

MY MUSIC DROWNED OUT THEIR WORDS.

I'VE WANTED CONCEALER SINCE I WAS AROUND 12.

I DAYDREAMED OF BEING RID OF MY UNDER-EYE CIRCLES.

I NERVOUSLY MILLED AROUND THE MAKEUP SHOP

TOO AFRAID TO ASK FOR HELP CHOOSING.

THE WOMAN WHO HELPED ME NEVER BATTED AN EYE.

A PERFECT ANGEL.

MAY 17TH, 2016

HOW AM I DOING?

AM I DOING BETTER?
AM I HAPPIER?

IT'S TOUGH TO QUANTIFY.

I THINK I HATE MYSELF LESS.
THAT'S NICE.

I'VE SURROUNDED MYSELF
WITH SUPPORTIVE FRIENDS.

I DON'T FEEL ALONE ANYMORE.
I'M NOT ALONE

MAY 18TH, 2016

I WENT OUT IN MY OLD CLOTHES FOR LASER.
(ILL-FITTING CUZ I LOST WEIGHT)
IT WAS.. UNCOMFORTABLE.
I GUESS I'VE GROWN USED TO BEING PERCEIVED BY SOCIETY IN A CERTAIN LIGHT.
TAKE A SEAT.
IT FELT WRONG HAVING HAD IT TAKEN AWAY.
I HADN'T REALIZED HOW IMPORTANT IT'S BECOME
FOR OTHERS TO SEE ME AS I SEE MYSELF.

MAY 21ST, 2016

"BACK WHEN I THOUGHT YOU WERE A GUY."

JANE'S OFFHAND COMMENT KEEPS BOUNCING IN MY HEAD.

I'M JUST SO FLOORED TO HAVE SURROUNDED MYSELF

WITH FRIENDS WHO SO READ-ILY ACCEPT THIS NEW ME.

WHAT A WONDERFUL LIFE.

I NEVER COULD HAVE IMAGINED.

MAY 22ND, 2016

HUNG OUT AT THE POOL
WITH THE FAMILY.

I DON'T GO SWIMMING,
I DON'T DARE WEAR
A SWIMSUIT.

BEAUTIFUL WOMEN

EVERYWHERE.

I'M SUDDENLY HYPER-
AWARE OF EVERYTHING
I HATE ABOUT MYSELF.

MAY 25TH, 2016

I'VE BEEN REMOVING MY OLD FB PICS

IT FEELS WEIRD TO DELETE THE PAST.

I'M FINE WITH THE PHOTOS THEMSELVES

I JUST DON'T WANT THEM REPRESENTING ME.

SO MANY SMALL, CUTE MOMENTS

SELINA: HOLY CRAP YOUR HAIR ALREADY GREW BACK MOSTLY

JAKE: HAIRHAIRHAIR NOW I KNOWWW

GRAHAM: ICE CREAMS FROM SPACEMENS!

FOREVER GONE.

JUNE 2ND, 2016

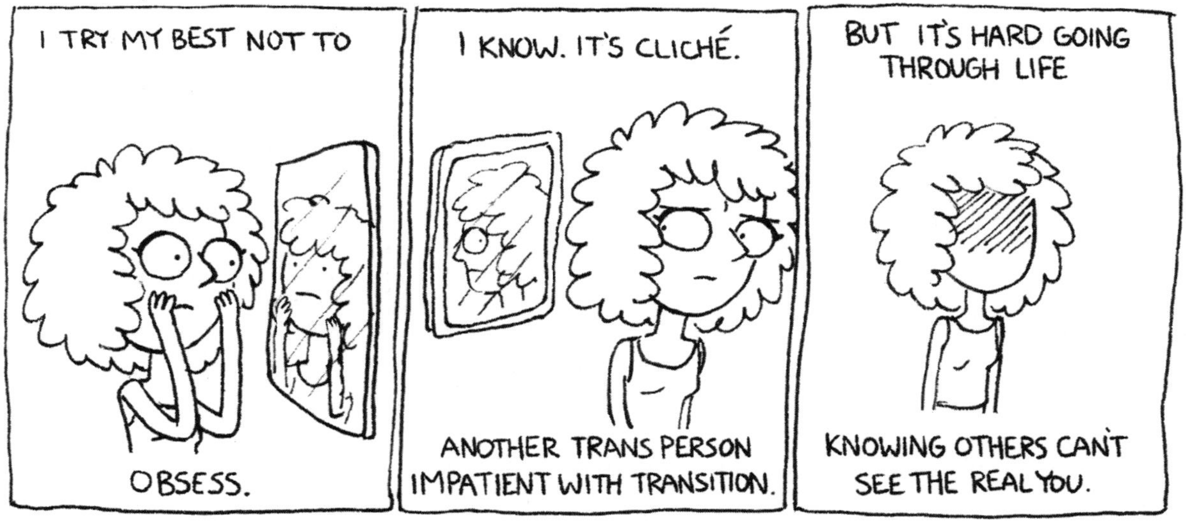
I TRY MY BEST NOT TO
OBSESS.
I KNOW. IT'S CLICHÉ.
ANOTHER TRANS PERSON IMPATIENT WITH TRANSITION.
BUT IT'S HARD GOING THROUGH LIFE
KNOWING OTHERS CAN'T SEE THE REAL YOU.

JUNE 3RD, 2016

I HATE HAVING TO
WOMEN
MEN
USE PUBLIC RESTROOMS.
I DON'T FEEL RIGHT USING THE WOMEN'S,
I DON'T WANT TO MAKE OTHERS UNCOMFORTABLE.
SO I USED THE MEN'S.
WHAT THE [redacted] IS THAT??
IT'S NOT ANY BETTER.

REMOVING MY MAKEUP IS THE WORST PART OF MY DAY.

SEEING MY FACE UNDERNEATH.

I WANT TO GO INTO A COMA,

ZZZ

WAKE ME UP IN A YEAR.

ANYTHING TO HASTEN

ESCAPING THIS HELL I'M IN.

JUNE 5TH, 2016

WEARING FEMME CLOTHES	AROUND MY PARENTS	IS STILL WEIRD.

JUNE 6TH, 2016

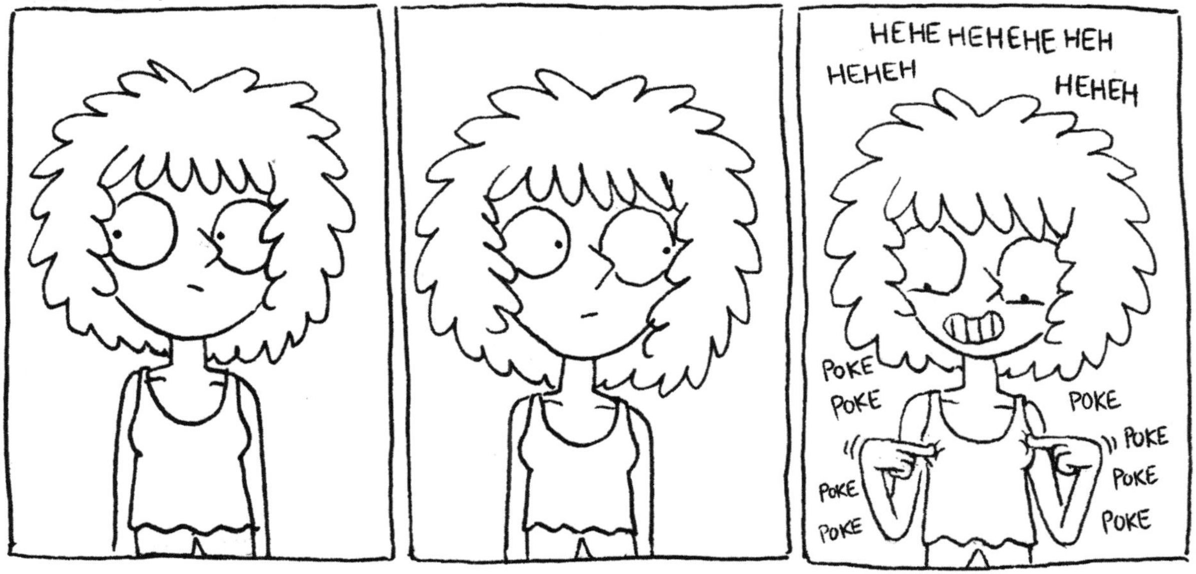
HEHE HEHEHE HEH
HEHEH
HEHEH
POKE
POKE
POKE
POKE
POKE
POKE
POKE
POKE
POKE

I MAY HAVE BEEN BORN INTO A

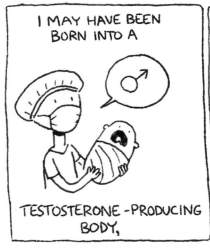

TESTOSTERONE - PRODUCING BODY,

I MAY LOOK MASCULINE,

I MAY SOUND MASCULINE,

BUT I AM MORE THAN THE SUM OF MY PARTS.

I'M A WOMAN.

JUNE 8TH, 2016

..AND YOU KNOW WHAT HE SAID?
SHE. WHAT SHE SAID.
MY PARENTS?
RIGHT, SHE. SHE LEFT THE VEGGIES IN THE FRIDGE. SHE THOUGHT..

JUNE 9TH, 2016

I FELT GOOD ABOUT MYSELF TODAY.

I WORKED HARD AND FELT GOOD.

AND THAT'S IMPORTANT.

JUNE 10TH, 2016

I USED A PUBLIC WOMEN'S RESTROOM.

SOMEONE CAME IN.

I WAS TOO NERVOUS TO COME OUT.

IT'S TAKEN ME AWHILE TO WARM UP TO IT BUT

MY SUPPORT GROUP HAS GROWN ON ME.

THEY'RE GOOD PEOPLE.

YES, JULIE?

I ACTUALLY SPEAK UP FROM TIME TO TIME

IT'S SO IMPORTANT TO BE AROUND OTHERS

WHO WALK THE SAME PATH.

JUNE 12TH, 2016

I'VE BEEN SEEING A WOMAN

IN THE MIRROR MORE OFTEN LATELY.

I'M STILL VISIBLY TRANS,

ALL THAT'S CHANGED IS MY MINDSET.

BEING NAMED AND GENDERED PROPERLY

HAS MADE A BIG IMPACT ON MY SELF-ACCEPTANCE.

JUNE 13TH, 2016

THE PEOPLE IN MY LIFE KNOW I'M FEMALE

AND IT'S OKAY.

I CAN WEAR WHAT I WANT & USE MAKEUP

AND IT'S OKAY.

I'VE WORKED PAST SO MUCH SELF-SHAME.

I STILL CAN'T BELIEVE HOW FAR I'VE COME.

JUNE 14TH, 2016

IT'S BEEN 2 MONTHS
..I'M TRANSGENDER.
SINCE I LAST SPOKE TO [redacted]
2 MONTHS
FOLLOW YOUR BLISS.
SINCE HE SAID HE WAS SUPPORTIVE.
HOW MANY MORE
BEFORE I HEAR FROM HIM AGAIN?

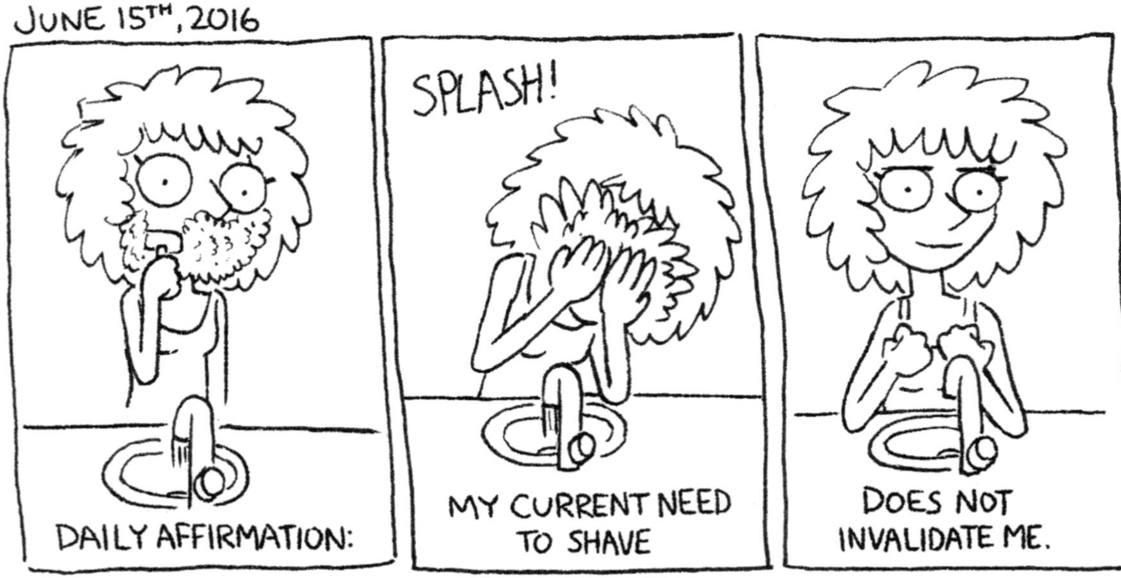
JUNE 15TH, 2016
DAILY AFFIRMATION:
SPLASH!
MY CURRENT NEED TO SHAVE
DOES NOT INVALIDATE ME.

JUNE 16TH, 2016

Panel 1:

A NEW HURDLE:

VISITING LOCAL BUSINESSES I FREQUENTED BEFORE GOING FULL-TIME.

Panel 2:

TO MY RELIEF THEY'VE ALL BEEN RESPECTFUL.

YOUR TOTAL COMES TO $13.75.

IT'S LIKE THERE WAS NO CHANGE AT ALL.

Panel 3:

I STILL AVOID SOME PLACES THOUGH.

CAFE

I WISH I COULD SHAKE MY FEARS.

JUNE 17TH, 2016

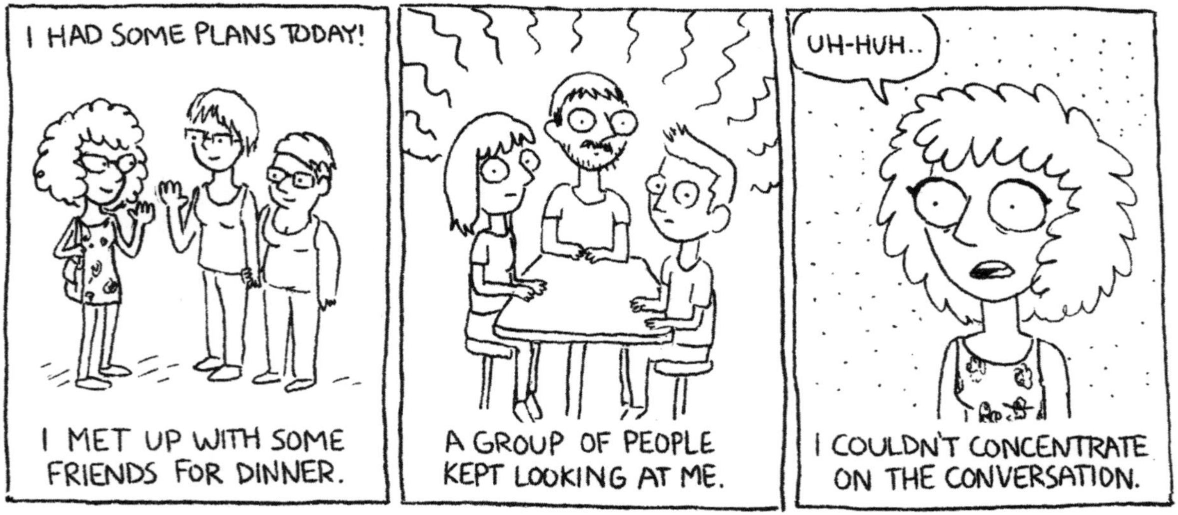
I HAD SOME PLANS TODAY!
I MET UP WITH SOME FRIENDS FOR DINNER.
A GROUP OF PEOPLE KEPT LOOKING AT ME.
UH-HUH..
I COULDN'T CONCENTRATE ON THE CONVERSATION.

EVERYONE IS GETTING TOGETHER TOMORROW FOR FATHER'S DAY.

WILL ████████ SHOW UP?

HE'S BEEN AVOIDING ME.

OUR RELATIONSHIP WAS GOOD BEFORE I CAME OUT.

SIGH.

I JUST DON'T GET IT. I'M STILL ME.

JUNE 19TH, 2016

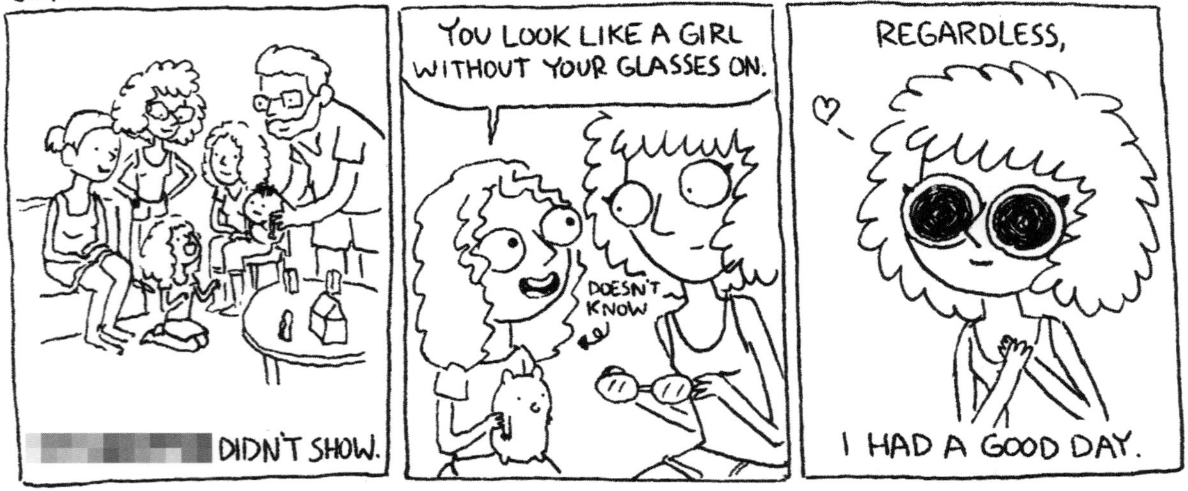
[redacted] DIDN'T SHOW.
YOU LOOK LIKE A GIRL WITHOUT YOUR GLASSES ON.
DOESN'T KNOW
REGARDLESS,
I HAD A GOOD DAY.

I USED TO BE SCARED OF BEING VISIBLY TRANS

BUT MOST PEOPLE DON'T SEEM TO CARE.

THE ONLY PERSON TO FEAR IS MYSELF.

I'M AN EXPERT AT CUTTING MYSELF DOWN.

I NEED TO BE PATIENT.

WHY CAN'T I SEEM TO LEARN THIS LESSON?

JUNE 21ST, 2016

I FELT REALLY CUTE TODAY, UNTIL..
THANK YOU, SIR.
"SIR."
I KNEW IT WAS BOUND TO HAPPEN OCCASIONALLY,
DO I.. SAY SOMETHING?
BUT I UNDERESTIMATED HOW INVALIDATING IT WOULD FEEL.
IS THAT HOW PEOPLE SEE ME? ARE THEY JUST HUMORING ME?
..HAVE A NICE DAY..
I NEED TO GROW A THICKER SKIN.

EVERY MORNING

BED HEAD

TUG TUG TUG TUG

I WAKE UP, PUT ON MY CLOTHES AND MAKEUP.

THE SHEEN HAS WORN OFF.

WET HAIR

IT'S BECOME ROUTINE.

IT'S.. NICE.

IT'S JUST MY LIFE NOW.

JUNE 23ᴿᴰ, 2016

I WENT OUT TODAY AND WAS SUDDENLY STRUCK WITH	I FELT INCREDIBLY CONSTRAINED BY THE	I TOOK OFF MY MAKEUP AND CLOTHES BUT
BEING UNCOMFORTABLE WITH MY OUTWARD PRESENTATION	 BOX I'VE PLACED MYSELF IN MARKED "FEMALE"	 IT DIDN'T HELP. I JUST FELT SO HELPLESS.

I DROVE MY MOM DOWN TO THE HAIR SALON.

NBD, OVER IT.

I'D BE COMING OUT TO A STYLIST I'D KNOWN FOR YEARS.

TURNED OUT SHE'D OUTED ME AGES AGO.

??? ??

HEY JULIE!

UH... HI??

"(m)"

WE'VE SPOKEN ABOUT BOUNDARIES IN THE PAST.

I TRIED TO EXPLAIN WHY HER ACTIONS HURT.

I'M JUST SO PROUD OF YOU.

MEANS WELL ➡

BUT SHE DIDN'T SEEM TO GET IT.

JUNE 26TH, 2016

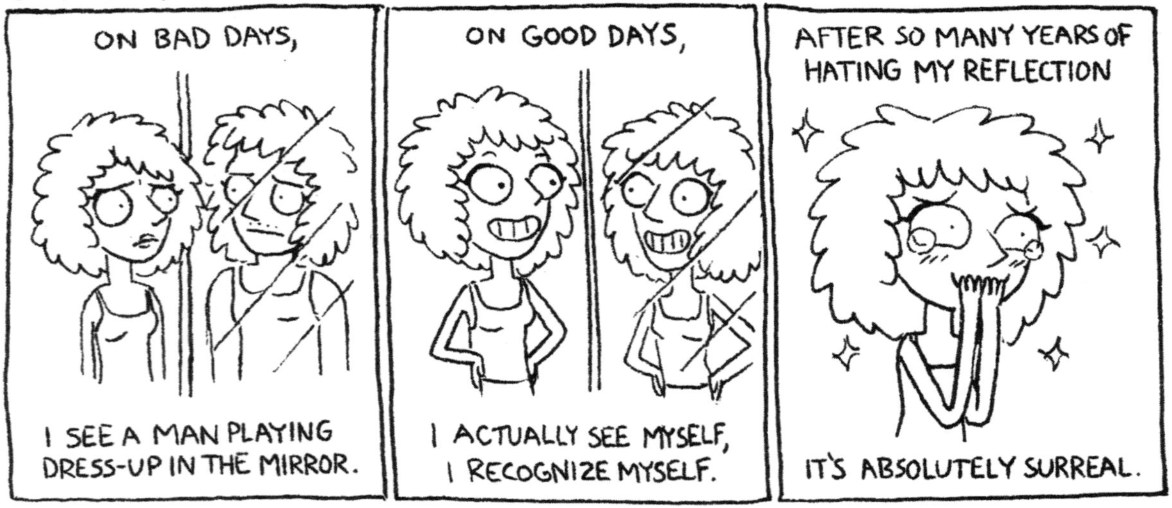
ON BAD DAYS,
I SEE A MAN PLAYING DRESS-UP IN THE MIRROR.
ON GOOD DAYS,
I ACTUALLY SEE MYSELF, I RECOGNIZE MYSELF.
AFTER SO MANY YEARS OF HATING MY REFLECTION
IT'S ABSOLUTELY SURREAL.

JUNE 27TH, 2016

I WENT TO THE STORE.

I NOTICED MY MISTAKE ALL TOO LATE.

I HAD FORGOTTEN TO WEAR A GAFF.

I STARTED THE NAME-CHANGE PROCESS!

DID I DO 'EM ALL??

I HAD TO SIFT THROUGH A LOT OF FORMS.

I WAS GREETED AT THE DOOR OF THE COURTHOUSE.

SECURITY

HELLO THERE, BEAUTIFUL!

VERY MIXED FEELINGS ABOUT THAT.

THE CLERKS WERE SO SWEET AND HELPFUL.

OH, YOU NEED ONE MORE FORM. LEMME GO AND PRINT ONE OUT FOR YA.

MY COURT DATE IS SET FOR NEXT MONTH.

JUNE 29TH, 2016

HAVING AN OFFICIAL DATE FOR MY NAME CHANGE IS INCREDIBLY VALIDATING.

I'LL SOON BE LEGALLY RECOGNIZED AS MY PROPER GENDER

GIRL.

BANG BANG

EXTERNAL VALIDATION CONTINUES TO PLAY A BIG ROLE IN MY SELF-ACCEPTANCE.

IS THAT GOOD? BAD?

WHO CARES!

JUNE 30TH, 2016

IT'S LIKE A SWITCH WAS FLIPPED IN MY BRAIN.
FLICK
THESE PAST FEW DAYS.
I'M MORE SECURE IN MY GENDER IDENTITY
THAN EVER BEFORE.
THERE ARE A FEW THINGS I NEED TO DO FIRST, BUT
HELLO, HR?
INFORMING COMPANY THAT HIRED ME
I'M FINALLY READY TO PUBLICLY COME OUT.

JULY 1ST, 2016

I'VE GONE THROUGH A DRESS PHASE RECENTLY.

A SYMBOL OF FEMININITY, IT WAS AN ARMOR I COULD WEAR TO REMIND MYSELF AND OTHERS I'M A GIRL.

NOW MORE SECURE IN MY GENDER IDENTITY, I DON'T FEEL A NEED TO WEAR 'EM. (BUT IT'S STILL A COOL OPTION!)

JULY 2ND, 2016

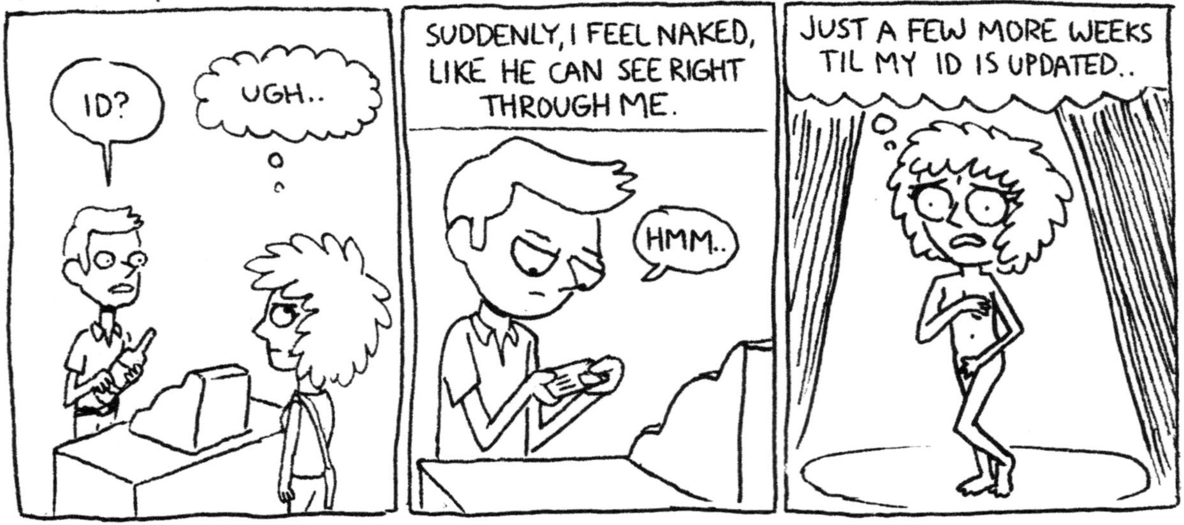
ID?
UGH..
SUDDENLY, I FEEL NAKED, LIKE HE CAN SEE RIGHT THROUGH ME.
HMM..
JUST A FEW MORE WEEKS TIL MY ID IS UPDATED..

JULY 3ʳᵈ, 2016

I'VE GOTTEN BETTER, BUT I'M STILL SO INSECURE IN MY OUTWARD GENDER EXPRESSION.

I COVER MY FACE IN MAKEUP TO HIDE FROM MY REFLECTION.

WITHOUT IT, I LOOK LIKE A MAN. I WISH I COULD SEE PAST IT, BUT I CAN'T.

DESPITE ANY MINOR PITFALLS I HAPPEN INTO REGULARLY, I'M NO LONGER DEPRESSED.

I'VE WORKED HARD TO CLIMB OUT OF THE HOLE I WAS IN FOR SO LONG.

AND I'M GOING TO KEEP WORKING HARD TO ENSURE I DON'T FALL BACK IN.

JULY 5TH, 2016

CLICK!

I FELT DOWN, SO I DECIDED TO RE-CREATE A PIC TAKEN OVER A YEAR AGO.

HA HA HA HA HA
HA HA HA
HA HA HA HAHA HA
HA

HA
HA
HA HA

I ENDED UP DOUBLED OVER WITH LAUGHTER TRYING TO MAKE THE SAME GOOFY FACE.

FIRST TIME WEARING FOUNDATION

6 MONTHS HRT

IT HIT HOME HOW FAR I'VE ALREADY COME

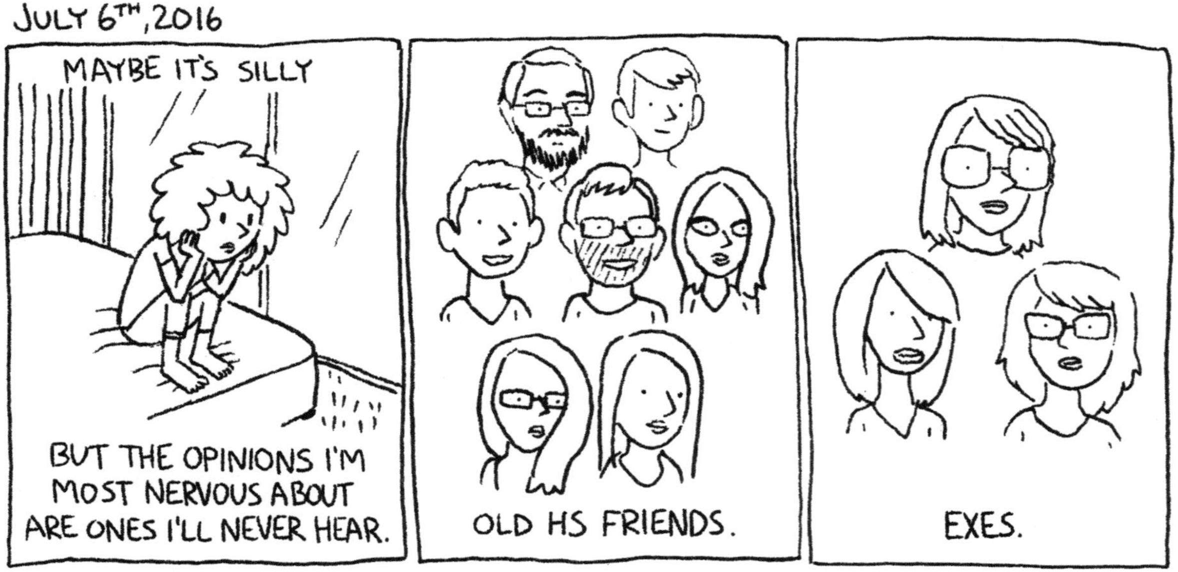
JULY 6TH, 2016
MAYBE IT'S SILLY
BUT THE OPINIONS I'M MOST NERVOUS ABOUT ARE ONES I'LL NEVER HEAR.
OLD HS FRIENDS.
EXES.

JULY 7TH, 2016

FACE LASER DAY.
NO MAKEUP, I FEEL SO
E X P O S E D.

THE CAFE WORKERS
KEEP GLANCING.
I FEEL EVERY LOOK.

I TEAR MYSELF DOWN.
I HATE MYSELF.

WHO ARE YOU?
YOU HELPED ME AT
THE STORE TODAY.

YOU SEEMED SO
COMFORTABLE IN
YOUR OWN SKIN.

I WISH I WAS
HALF AS CONFIDENT.

JULY 9TH, 2016

TRANSITIONING HAS BEEN THE MOST EXHAUSTING EXPERIENCE OF MY LIFE.

A NEVER-ENDING MARATHON OF NEW EXPERIENCES BOTH GOOD AND BAD.

I FEEL LIKE I'M RUNNING OUT OF STEAM, BUT I HAVE TO KEEP PUSHING MYSELF FORWARD.

JULY 11TH, 2016

TOMORROW I TALK TO
HR, THE FINAL HURDLE
BEFORE I CAN FINALLY
BE OUT PUBLICLY.

OH MY GOD.
THIS IS A
REAL THING
THAT I'M
GONNA GO
THROUGH.

A YEAR AGO I NEVER
COULD HAVE IMAGINED
BEING STRONG ENOUGH
TO GET TO THIS POINT.

SHHHHH

I WISH I COULD GO BACK
TO HUG AND TELL MYSELF
IT'LL ALL BE OKAY.
I'LL BE OKAY.

JULY 12TH, 2016

PUSH

COMING OUT DAY.
IT TOOK AN ETERNITY
TO HIT SEND.

TYPE TYPE

HEHEHE
HEHE

MY FRIEND DAN
DISTRACTED ME,
CALMING MY NERVES.

ALL AFTERNOON I WAS
INUNDATED WITH LOVE
AND SUPPORT FROM
FRIENDS AND STRANGERS.

OLD HS FRIENDS CONTACTED ME IN SUPPORT OF MY COMING OUT.

HAD I KNOWN BACK THEN, THEY WOULD'VE BEEN THERE FOR ME.

A BEAUTIFUL THOUGHT.

JULY 14TH, 2016

THE DUST HAS SETTLED.
EVERYONE KNOWS.
THE WORLD DIDN'T END

TYPE
TYPE

LIFE IS SO NORMAL
THAT IT'S AS IF
NOTHING'S CHANGED.

I SUPPOSE NOTHING HAS.
AND THAT'S GREAT.

JULY 16TH, 2016

I HAD HUNG OUT WITH THIS GROUP PRETRANSITION SO THEY HAD TO ADJUST.

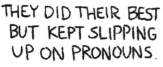

THEY DID THEIR BEST BUT KEPT SLIPPING UP ON PRONOUNS.

LET IT SLIDE, THEY'RE TRYING. LET IT SLIDE.

JULY 17TH, 2016

AT THE SUPERMARKET
AN OLD MAN WAS
GAWPING RELENTLESSLY.

I STARED HIM IN THE
EYE UNTIL HE FINALLY
TURNED IN SHAME.

IT SHOULDN'T HAVE
TO COME TO THAT.

JULY 18TH, 2016

I WENT OUT TO A SHOW IN BOYMODE.

IT WAS.. NICE. I FELT INVISIBLE.

I MISS IT SO MUCH. MY LIFE IS EXHAUSTING.

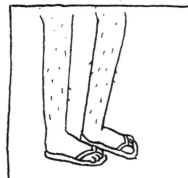

I HAVEN'T SHAVED
MY LEGS IN 3 DAYS.
WHO CARES.

I WENT OUT TODAY,
PEOPLE LOOKED.
LET 'EM STARE.

I FELT POWERFUL.

ONE OF MY COUSINS
MESSAGED ME IN
SUPPORT OF MY
TRANSITION.

SHE'S THE FIRST
OF MY RELATIVES
TO DO SO.

I ALSO STARTED THE
LEGAL NAME-CHANGE
FILING PROCESS!

I'VE REALIZED I'VE COME TO LIKE MY REFLECTION MORE OFTEN THAN NOT.

MY BODY ISN'T PERFECT, AND I'LL NEVER HAVE A PETITE FRAME.

INSTEAD, I'M A BEAUTIFUL GIANT.

MY BODY DYSPHORIA LESSENED FOR NOW, MY THOUGHTS SHIFT TO MY VOICE: LOW. DEEP.

HELLO THERE

I NEED TO PRACTICE MORE. I DON'T PUT ENOUGH EFFORT IN. IT GRATES ON MY EARS.

OH YOU SHOULD'VE BEEN A MOTHER, SHOULD'VE BEEN A WIFE

BUT SINGING ALONG WITH LAURA JANE GRACE MAKES ME FEEL LESS BROKEN.

JULY 23ᴿᴰ, 2016

IT WAS AN AWFUL
SELF-IMAGE DAY.

I DECIDED TO BOOST MY
CONFIDENCE BY DOING
MYSELF UP ALL PURTY.

IT WORKED.

CLICK
CLICK
CLICK

HEY THERE
GOOD LOOKIN'.

TIME FOR MY FIRST PAIR OF FEMME SHOES!

SALE

THE FIRST STORE DIDN'T EVEN CARRY MY SIZE.

MY LONG/WIDE FEET MEAN A MORE.. LIMITED SELECTION.

CLEARANCE SHOES

DIDN'T STOP ME FROM FINDING SOME CUTIES AT STORE #2!

JULY 25TH, 2016

I DON'T LOOK LIKE ████████ ANYMORE

I MEAN:

I CAN BE UNHAPPY I LOOK MANNISH, BUT I NO LONGER THINK OF MYSELF AS A MAN.

I JUST SEE JULIA WAITING FOR HER BODY TO DEVELOP.

RIGHT THIS WAY, SIR.

'KAY.

IT DIDN'T GET TO ME. NOT RIGHT AWAY.

I LATER SPENT AN HOUR STARING IN THE MIRROR, SELF-HATING.

JULY 27TH, 2016

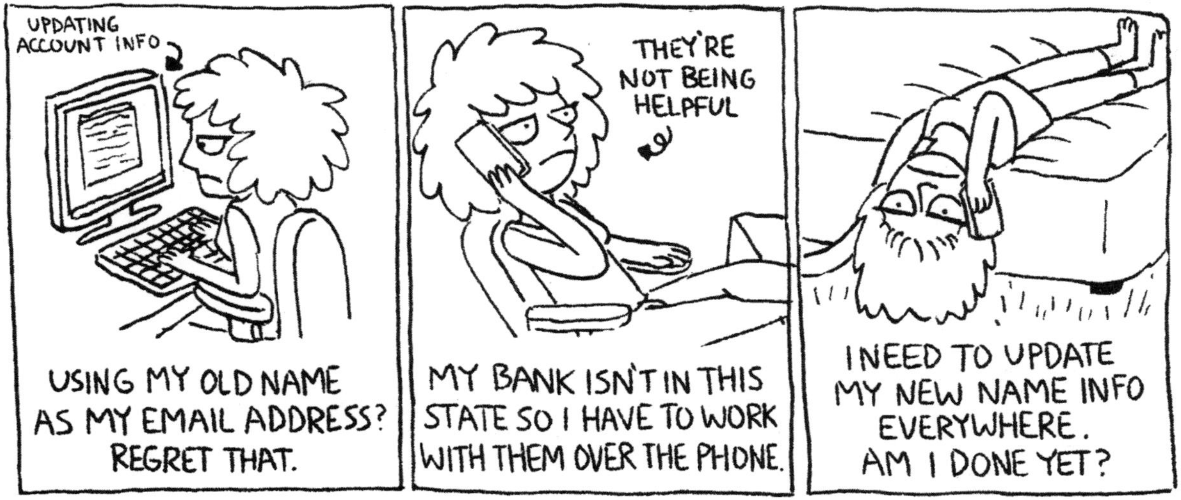
UPDATING ACCOUNT INFO
USING MY OLD NAME AS MY EMAIL ADDRESS? REGRET THAT.
THEY'RE NOT BEING HELPFUL
MY BANK ISN'T IN THIS STATE SO I HAVE TO WORK WITH THEM OVER THE PHONE.
I NEED TO UPDATE MY NEW NAME INFO EVERYWHERE. AM I DONE YET?

JULY 28TH, 2016

SCORE! 0.2 lbs LIGHTER!

ON SCALE 5TH TIME THAT DAY

MY WEIGHT DROPPED DUE TO BODY DYSPHORIA EARLIER THIS YEAR.

I HATED MY BODY AND NEEDED TO CHANGE IT THE ONLY WAY I COULD CONTROL.

HM.

..MAYBE JUST A QUICK CHECK.

ALREADY CHECKED TODAY

I'M NOW BACK TO A HEALTHIER WEIGHT BUT STILL STRUGGLE AGAINST BAD HABITS.

Panel 1:
HM.. IT'S TIME.

I POSTED A PIC OF MYSELF ONLINE. A FEW SAID I LOOKED CIS??

Panel 2:
MAYBE IF I SQUINT..

AND TURN MY HEAD..

A VERY STRANGE THING TO HEAR. I HONESTLY CAN'T SEE IT.

Panel 3:
SEX*:F

*GENDER

ALSO! I GOT MY GENDER MARKER CHANGED! I'M LEGALLY A LADY NOW.

I DON'T KNOW HOW TO DEAL WITH ONLINE TRANSPHOBIA.

SURE, I CAN BLOCK THEM, BUT THEIR MESSAGE HAS ALREADY REACHED ME.

"YOU SHOULDN'T EXIST."

JULY 31st, 2016

UNTIL THIS PAST YEAR, I LIVED MY ENTIRE LIFE APPEARING AS A STRAIGHT WHITE CISGENDER MALE.

I WAS NEVER DISCRIMINATED AGAINST. I WAS INVISIBLE.

IT'S NEW TO ME, BUT I'LL LEARN TO DEAL. I'LL GROW A THICKER SKIN.

AUGUST 1ST, 2016

I JUST WANTED TO SAY. THAT YOU'RE GORGEOUS.

COMPLIMENTS ARE HARD FOR ME TO ACCEPT, NO MATTER WHO SAYS 'EM TO ME.

OH, THANKS!

..FOR A TRANS-GIRL, YOU MEAN.

MY IMMEDIATE REACTION IS TO THINK THAT THEY'RE JUST TRYING TO BE SUPPORTIVE.

MAYBE ONE DAY I'LL BE..

MY INSECURITIES GET IN THE WAY. I NEED TO START TRUSTING PEOPLE.

AUGUST 2ND, 2016

DRESS
PROBABLY
A LIL
TOO
SHORT

I WAS SUPER
BODY POSITIVE TODAY.

CONSCIOUSLY ACKNOWLEDGING
MY INSECURITIES SEEMS
TO HAVE HELPED (FOR NOW).

TRUSTING OTHERS CAN BE
SCARY, BUT IF OTHERS SAY
I'M PRETTY, MAYBE I AM.

LASER'S BEEN GOING WELL! BUUUUUUT~

GKKK

THE SETTING'S SO HIGH NOW, IT FEELS LIKE A SEWING MACHINE BEING USED ON MY BONES.

WORTH IT.

AUGUST 4TH, 2016
SO HOW'S [redacted]?
I HATE LYING
OH, UHH.. HE'S BEEN REALLY WELL!
BUT I SHOULDN'T BRING IT UP.
WWORKIN' HARD, YA KNOW? HEHEH
WHY AM I LYING FOR HIM

AUGUST 5TH, 2016

I SAW MY
THERAPIST TODAY.

IT'S OKAY TO FEEL
HURT BY ██████'S
ACTIONS.

IT'S OKAY TO FEEL ANGER.

AUGUST 6TH, 2016

CAN I GET A PRICE CHECK ON THESE MEN'S SOCKS?
ON MEN'S SOCKS??
YEAH MEN'S SOCKS!

AUGUST 7TH, 2016

MY NIECE'S BIRTHDAY PARTY. THE WHOLE FAMILY CAME.

██████ KEEPS AS FAR AWAY FROM ME AS POSSIBLE.

I PLAY WITH MY PHONE AS A DISTRACTION TO KEEP FROM CRYING.

AUGUST 8TH, 2016

FOR A WEEK AFTER LASER IT'S IMPOSSIBLE TO GET ANYTHING RESEMBLING A CLOSE SHAVE.

I PILE ON THE CONCEALER, BUT IT'S STILL OBVIOUSLY THERE.

LOOKING IN THE MIRROR IS LIKE A PUNCH TO THE GUT, BUT I CAN'T STOP MYSELF.

AUGUST 9TH, 2016

IN A MOMENT
OF CLARITY..

OH
DANG~

MY FEATURES I VIEW
AS MANNISH ARE JUST
STRONG AND ANGULAR.

HEY
MEGAN!

I LATER WENT ON A
HANGOUT WITHOUT
MAKEUP AND FELT
FINE. THAT'S NEW.

AUGUST 10TH, 2016

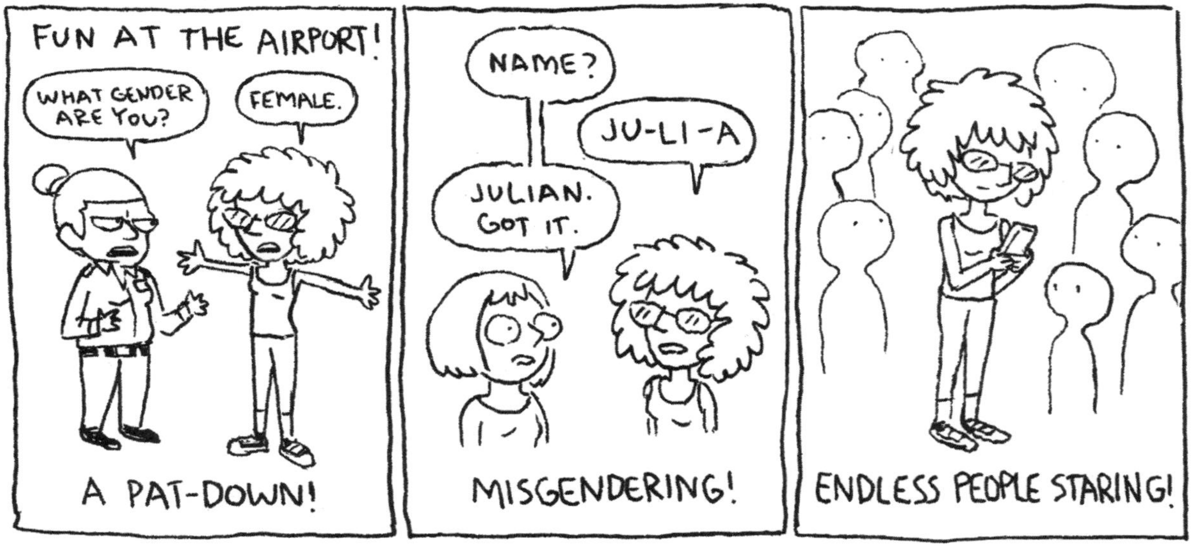
FUN AT THE AIRPORT!
WHAT GENDER ARE YOU?
FEMALE.
A PAT-DOWN!
NAME?
JU-LI-A
JULIAN. GOT IT.
MISGENDERING!
ENDLESS PEOPLE STARING!

AUGUST 10TH, 2016

IT'S BEEN A FEW DAYS
SHY OF A YEAR SINCE
I TOLD MY EX MY NEED
TO TRANSITION.

JUST ABOUT A YEAR
SINCE WE ENDED OUR
4-YEAR RELATIONSHIP.

A YEAR SINCE I'VE
SEEN HER IN PERSON.
I'M FLYING OUT TO MY
GOOD FRIEND RIGHT NOW.

AUGUST 11TH, 2016

TODAY'S BEEN INTENSE AND CATHARTIC. WE WERE BOTH ABLE TO SHARE OUR HURT.

SNIFF

WE HAD LEARNED SO MUCH OVER THE COURSE OF OUR RELATIONSHIP.

CLINK

THERE ARE NO REGRETS. I'M SO LUCKY TO HAVE HER BACK IN MY LIFE.

AUGUST 12TH, 2016

I'M AT A CONVENTION. STRANGELY, I DON'T FEEL ANXIOUS.

NOBODY'S BEEN RUDE. NOBODY'S BEEN STARING.

PEOPLE HAVE TOLD ME I'M BEAUTIFUL.

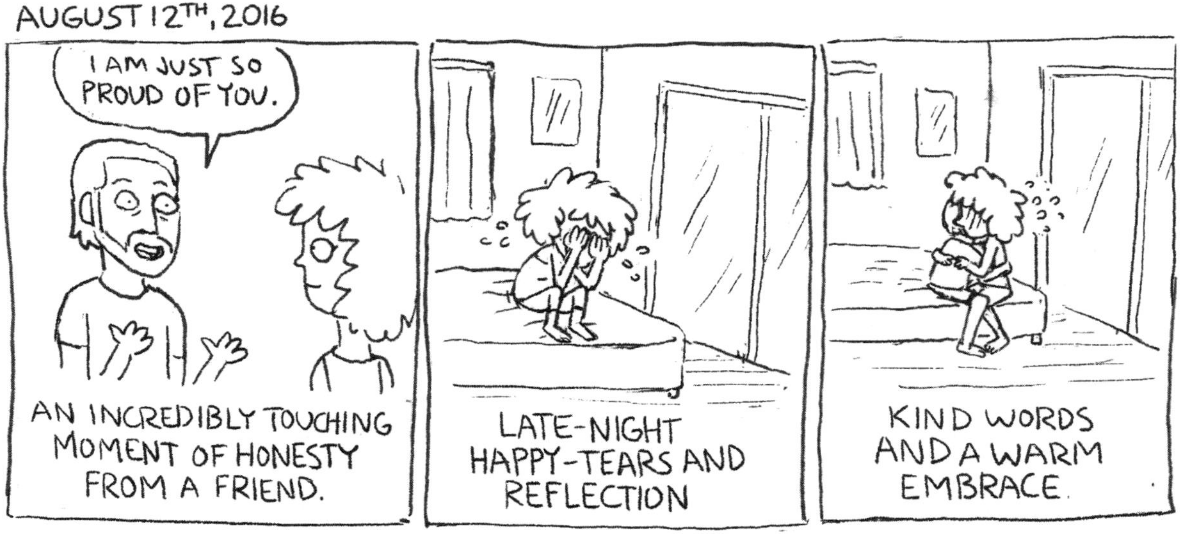
AUGUST 12TH, 2016
I AM JUST SO PROUD OF YOU.
AN INCREDIBLY TOUCHING MOMENT OF HONESTY FROM A FRIEND.
LATE-NIGHT HAPPY-TEARS AND REFLECTION
KIND WORDS AND A WARM EMBRACE.

AUGUST 13TH, 2016

SO, HOW'VE THINGS BEEN GOING FOR YA?

I'M ALWAYS HESITANT TO TALK ABOUT MY EXPERIENCES BEING TRANS WITH OTHERS.

HM. WHAT'S THE SOCIALLY ACCEPTABLE AMOUNT I CAN SAY WITHOUT FEELING LIKE I'M LYING?

I WORRY ABOUT BURDENING CONVERSATIONS, SO I TEND TO KEEP IT ALL TO MYSELF.

HOURS LATER

OH JEEZ, I'M GONNA CRY.

THAT'S OKAY!

BUT LAST NIGHT I FELT AT EASE OPENING UP TO A NEW FRIEND. IT WAS NICE.

AUGUST 14TH, 2016

BEFORE LEAVING THE CON, I TOOK A BUNCH OF PICS WITH FRIENDS FOR MEMORIES.

SEEMED LIKE A GREAT IDEA, BUT SEEING WHAT I ACTUALLY LOOK LIKE HURTS.

SIGH.

I HATE MY FACE SO MUCH IT'S PAINFUL.

AUGUST 16TH, 2016

I TEND TO ENGAGE IN

BLACK & WHITE THINKING.

I FELT GREAT TODAY, BUT

I'M EITHER ON TOP OF THE WORLD OR BEING CRUSHED BY IT.

I GUESS I'M STARTING TO RECOGNIZE

I NEED TO WORK ON SEEING SHADES OF GRAY.

AUGUST 17TH, 2016

CIS WOMEN CAN HAVE DEEP VOICES AND NOBODY QUESTIONS THEIR FEMININITY.

I KEEP THINKING BACK TO THAT CONVERSATION A FEW DAYS AGO.

YOU DON'T HAVE TO CHANGE YOURS.

HM.

MAYBE MY DYSPHORIA STEMS FROM INTERNALIZED TRANSPHOBIA.

MAYBE I DON'T NEED TO RAISE THE PITCH OF MY VOICE.

I'M NOT LESS OF A WOMAN FOR IT.

AUGUST 18TH, 2016

CAN I WEAR THIS WITHOUT BEING CALLED "SIR"?
DOES IT OBSCURE MY CHEST TOO MUCH?
IS THIS ENOUGH MAKEUP?
I HATE FEELING OBLIGATED, BUT I HATE BEING MISGENDERED MORE.
CAN I HELP YOU, MISS?
HOW MANY OF MY ACTIONS ARE JUST DEFENSE MECHANISMS?

WHEN I STARTED THERAPY
11 MONTHS AGO, I WAS
AN ANXIOUS WRECK.

I'M MOVING TO ANOTHER
STATE. TODAY WAS MY
LAST APPOINTMENT.

THINGS AREN'T PERFECT,
BUT I'VE COME SO FAR.

AUGUST 20TH, 2016

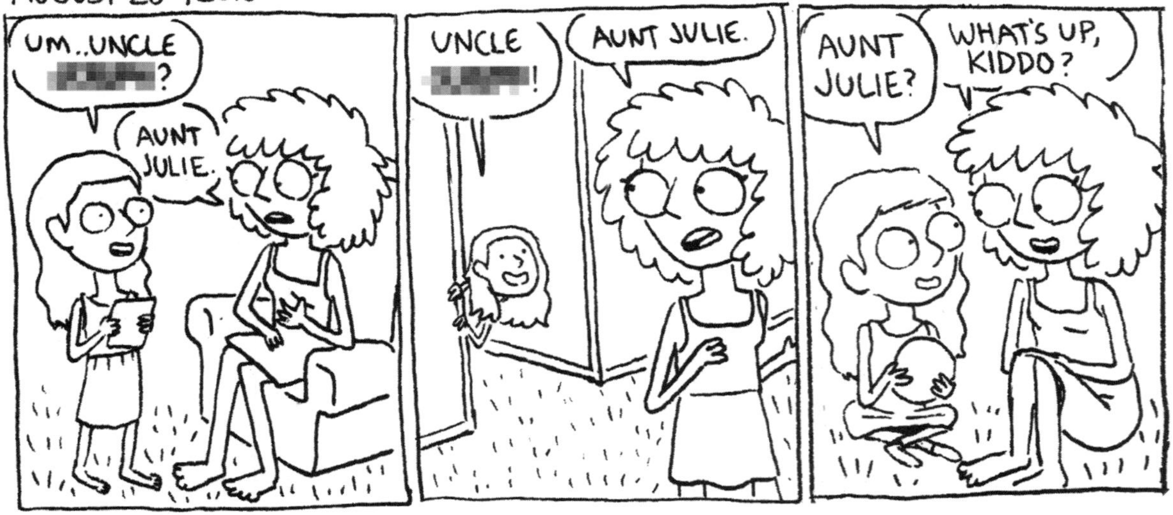
UM..UNCLE [redacted]?
AUNT JULIE.
UNCLE [redacted]!
AUNT JULIE.
AUNT JULIE?
WHAT'S UP, KIDDO?

AUGUST 21ST, 2016

MOMENTS

...OH.

CLEARING OUT THE CLOSET OF PRETRANSITION CLOTHES.

WHY COULDN'T I JUST HAVE BEEN HAPPY LIVING AS A GUY??

A SPIRAL OF DEPRESSION AFTER WATCHING OLD VIDEOS OF MYSELF.

I WENT OUT SHOPPING WITHOUT MAKEUP ON AND WAS OKAY (ISH).

AUGUST 22ND, 2016

I'M TIRED OF SELF-IMPOSED CONSTRAINTS.

I'M TRANSITIONING TO BE HAPPIER WITH MYSELF.

KICK!

GONNA BE MY OWN SPECIAL BRAND OF GIRL.

AUGUST 23RD, 2016

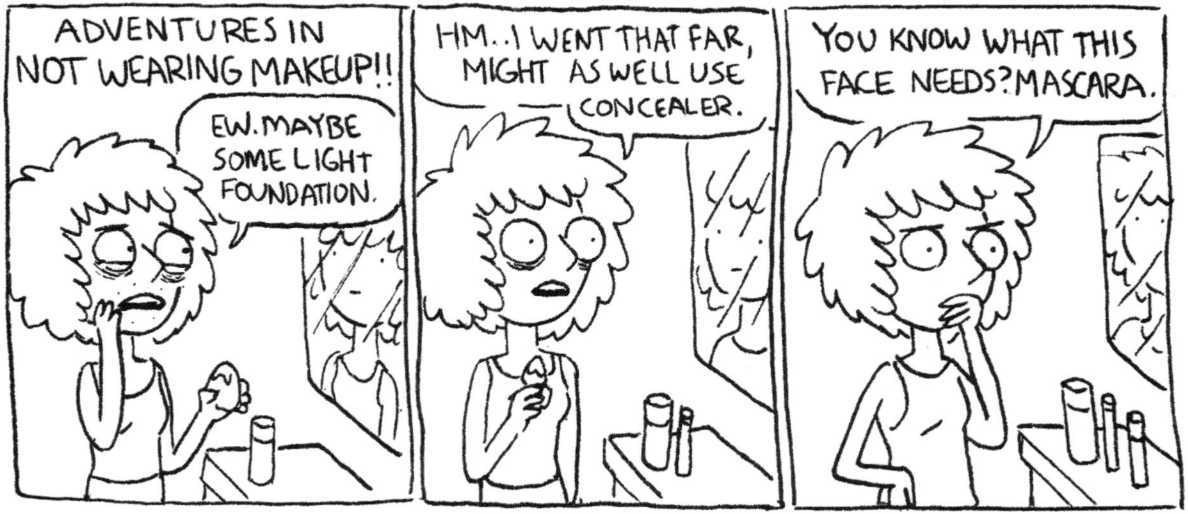
ADVENTURES IN NOT WEARING MAKEUP!!
EW. MAYBE SOME LIGHT FOUNDATION.
HM..I WENT THAT FAR, MIGHT AS WELL USE
CONCEALER.
YOU KNOW WHAT THIS FACE NEEDS? MASCARA.

AUGUST 24TH, 2016

I CONSTANTLY WORRY THAT PEOPLE IN PUBLIC JUST SEE ME AS A CROSS-DRESSING MAN.

WHOA HEY NOW!

I'M TRYING MY BEST TO WEAR WHAT I WANT AND NOT CARE.

BUT THE THOUGHT IS ALWAYS THERE.

AUGUST 25TH, 2016

I'VE BEEN WORRYING TOO MUCH ABOUT GENDER LATELY, FOCUSING TOO MUCH ON IT.

SNFFF

I JUST NEED TO CHILL OUT, RELAX.

WHEW~

EVERYTHING WILL FALL INTO PLACE IN TIME.

AUGUST 27TH, 2016

FOUND A JOURNAL

I WAS STILL HEAVILY QUESTIONING MY IDENTITY UP UNTIL THIS PAST JANUARY.

SIGH~

THAT WAS ONLY 8 MONTHS AGO. IT'S HARD TO IMAGINE AT THIS POINT.

LIVING LIFE AS A WOMAN JUST FEELS SO RIGHT.

AUGUST 28TH, 2016

I FEEL SO **VISIBLE** IN PUBLIC.

WHAT ARE THEY THINKING WHEN THEY SEE ME?

JUST FOCUS ON THE MUSIC..

I ALWAYS ASSUME THE WORST.

AUGUST 29TH, 2016

 JULIA KAYE
@UPANDOUTCOMIC

I SHOULD GO TO BED EARLY TONIGHT, SHE THINKS TO HERSELF AT 1 AM

8/29/16, 12:54AM

ılı VIEW ∿∿∿

USING FEMALE PRONOUNS ONLINE STILL FEELS DISINGENUOUS

IT FEELS LIKE A PUT-ON, LIKE I HAVEN'T EARNED IT.

WHAT A LOAD OF CRAP.

AUGUST 30ᵀᴴ, 2016

WHY DO I HAVE DAYS WHERE ALL I SEE IN THE MIRROR IS A MAN LOOKING BACK AT ME?

HE WASN'T THERE YESTERDAY.

SIGH..

I WISH HE'D GO AWAY.

AUGUST 31ˢᵀ, 2016

I'VE NOTICED THAT I
TURN AWAY FROM MY
NEIGHBORS WHEN
WALKING BY.

ACTUALLY
DID THIS
EARLIER

I EXPEND
TOO MUCH ENERGY
BEING REFLEXIVELY
ON MY GUARD.

THIS IS NO WAY TO
LIVE. I NEED TO TRUST
THAT MOST PEOPLE
WON'T BE AWFUL.

I'M MOVING TO A NEW CITY SOON.

NOBODY WILL HAVE KNOWN ME PRE TRANSITION.

I CAN'T WAIT.

SEPTEMBER 2ND, 2016

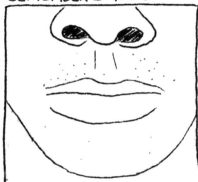

THE BEARD SHADOW ON MY UPPER LIP WAS REALLY GETTING TO ME.

I ENDED UP OVER-SHAVING TO TRY TO MINIMIZE IT.

CRUD.

NOW I HAVE RAZOR BURN AND IT'S MORE NOTICEABLE.

I LIVED FOR SO LONG AS A MAN, IT CAN BE HARD TO SHAKE THE IDEA THAT I'M NOT ONE??

I TRY TO BRUSH IT OFF, BUT IT'S SO INVALIDATING. IT MAKES ME FEEL FAKE.

I'VE COME SO FAR AND YET STILL HAVE SO FAR TO GO. I JUST WANT TO FEEL RIGHT.

SEPTEMBER 4TH, 2016

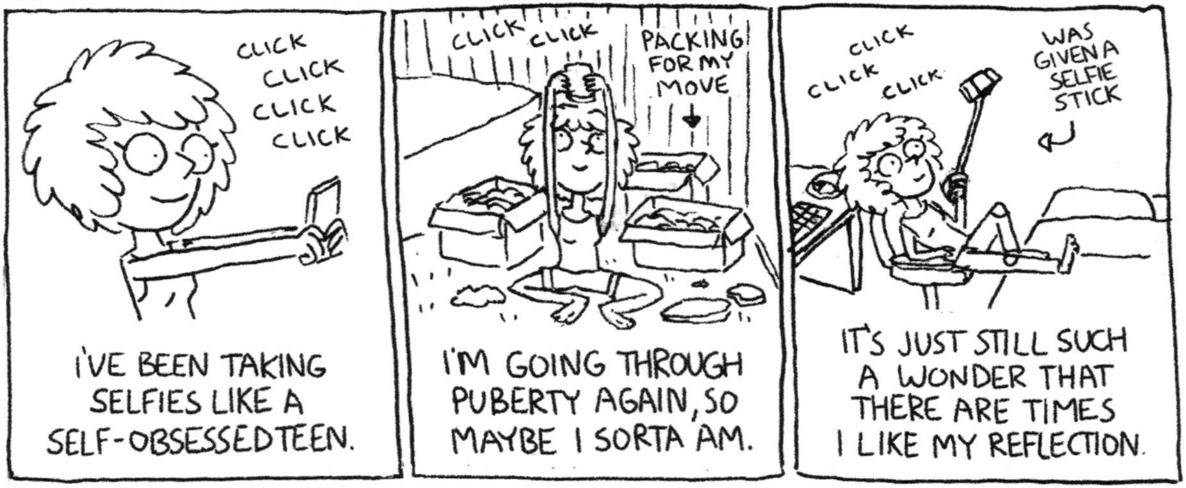
CLICK
CLICK
CLICK
CLICK
I'VE BEEN TAKING SELFIES LIKE A SELF-OBSESSED TEEN.
CLICK CLICK
PACKING FOR MY MOVE
I'M GOING THROUGH PUBERTY AGAIN, SO MAYBE I SORTA AM.
CLICK
CLICK
CLICK
WAS GIVEN A SELFIE STICK
IT'S JUST STILL SUCH A WONDER THAT THERE ARE TIMES I LIKE MY REFLECTION.

SEPTEMBER 5TH, 2016

I'VE BEEN CLOISTERED AWAY IN MY PARENTS' HOME ALL THIS TIME.

TOMORROW I MOVE, LEAVING MY COMFORT ZONE FOR GOOD.

BRING IT.

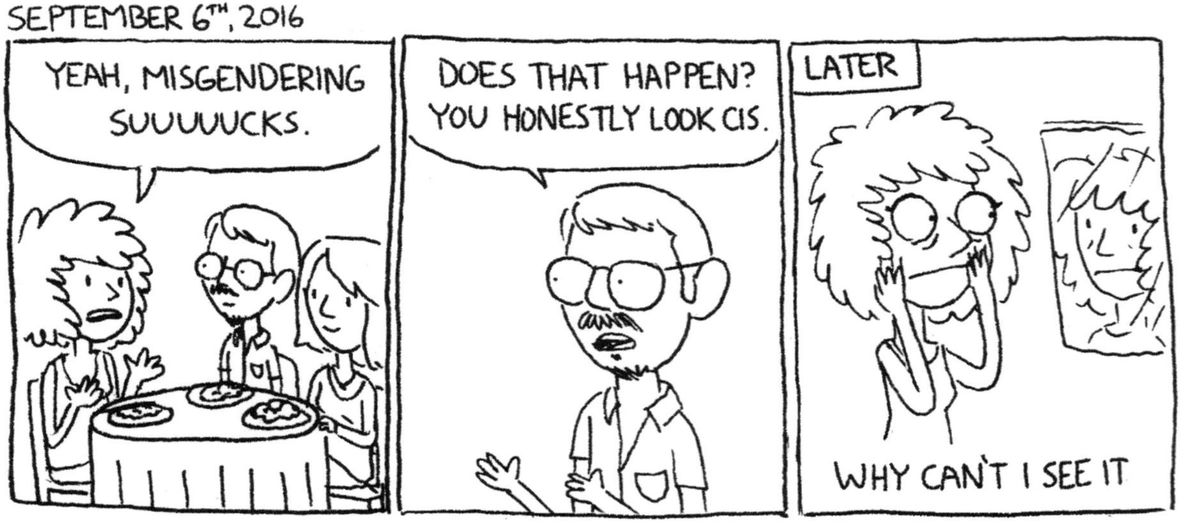
SEPTEMBER 6TH, 2016
YEAH, MISGENDERING SUUUUUCKS.
DOES THAT HAPPEN? YOU HONESTLY LOOK CIS.
LATER
WHY CAN'T I SEE IT

SEPTEMBER 7TH, 2016

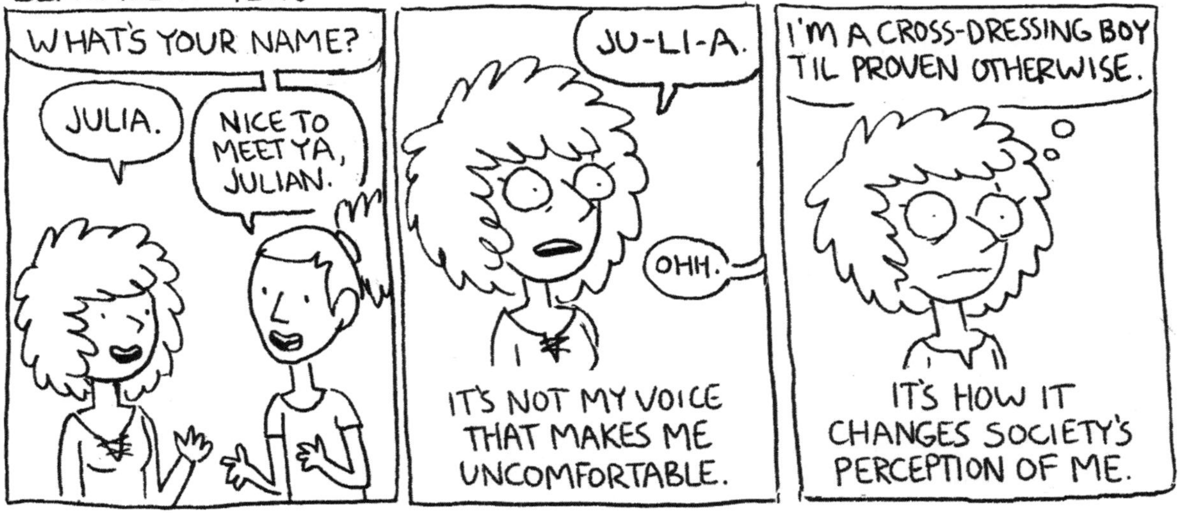
WHAT'S YOUR NAME?
JULIA.
NICE TO MEET YA, JULIAN.
JU-LI-A.
OHH.
IT'S NOT MY VOICE THAT MAKES ME UNCOMFORTABLE.
I'M A CROSS-DRESSING BOY TIL PROVEN OTHERWISE.
IT'S HOW IT CHANGES SOCIETY'S PERCEPTION OF ME.

SEPTEMBER 8TH, 2016

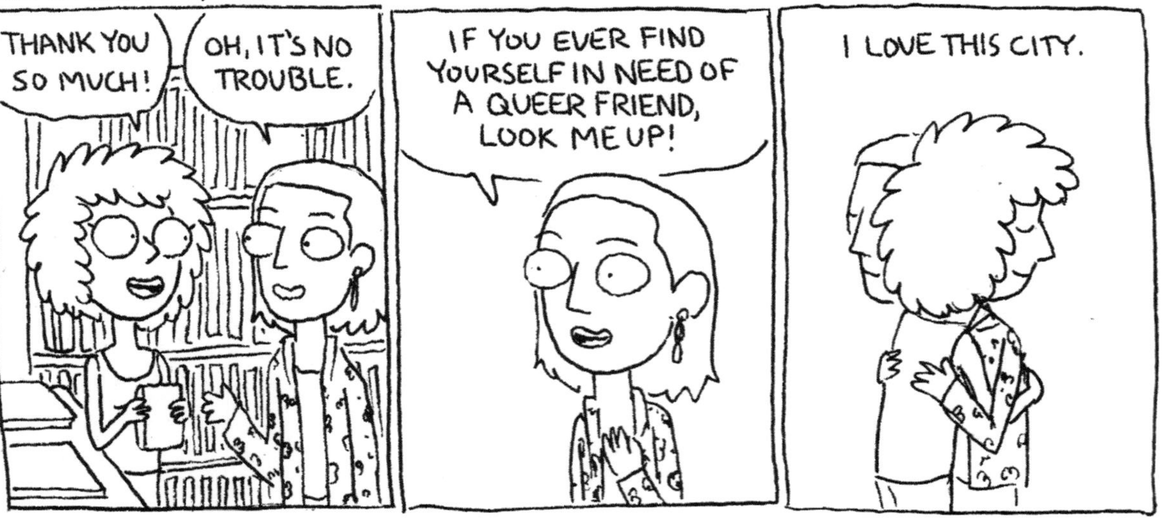
THANK YOU SO MUCH!
OH, IT'S NO TROUBLE.
IF YOU EVER FIND YOURSELF IN NEED OF A QUEER FRIEND, LOOK ME UP!
I LOVE THIS CITY.

SEPTEMBER 9TH, 2016

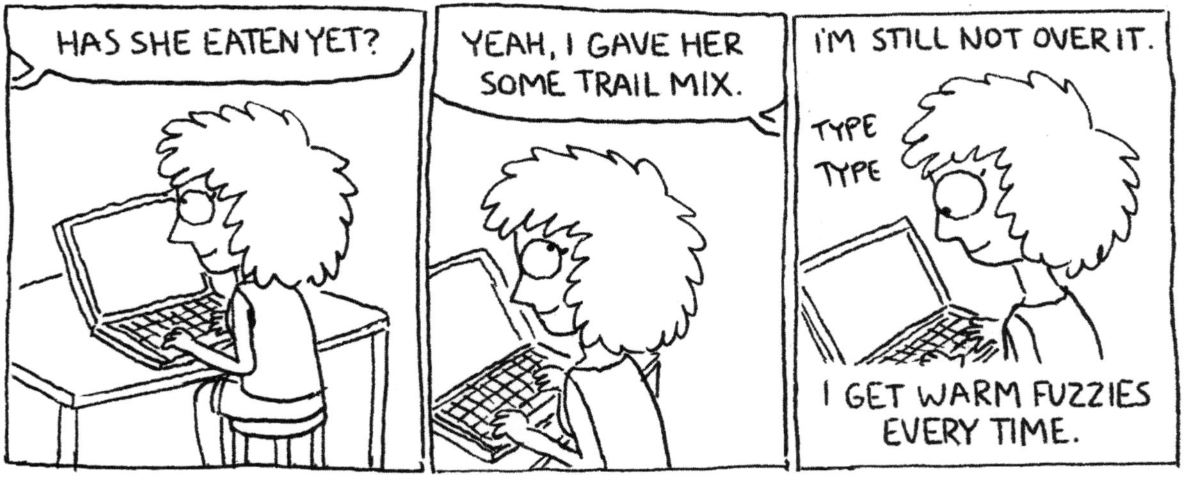
HAS SHE EATEN YET?
YEAH, I GAVE HER SOME TRAIL MIX.
I'M STILL NOT OVER IT.
TYPE
TYPE
I GET WARM FUZZIES EVERY TIME.

SEPTEMBER 10TH, 2016

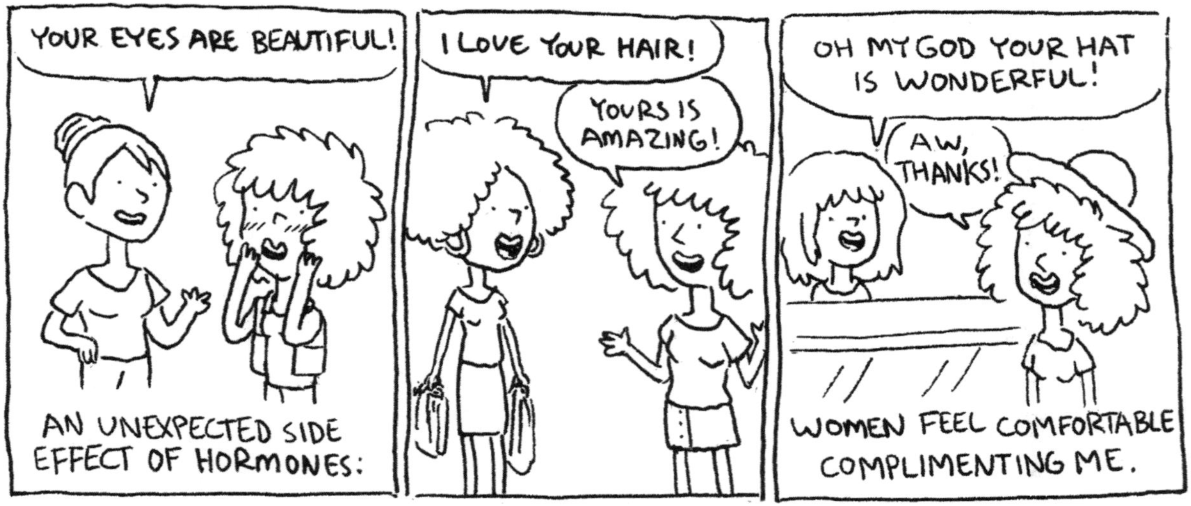
YOUR EYES ARE BEAUTIFUL!
AN UNEXPECTED SIDE EFFECT OF HORMONES:
I LOVE YOUR HAIR!
YOURS IS AMAZING!
OH MY GOD YOUR HAT IS WONDERFUL!
AW, THANKS!
WOMEN FEEL COMFORTABLE COMPLIMENTING ME.

SEPTEMBER 11TH, 2016

HEY MAN.
WHAT'S UP, MAN
YEAH, MAN
OVER HERE, MAN
WAY TO GO, MAN
REMEMBER:
YOU'RE IN CALIFORNIA, THEY DON'T MEAN ANYTHING BY IT.

SEPTEMBER 12TH, 2016

SALE!

I'VE BEEN THROUGH SO MUCH THIS PAST YEAR I OFTEN DON'T APPRECIATE HOW FAR I'VE COME.

MY EXTERIOR ACTUALLY REFLECTS WHO I AM. (MOSTLY, ANYWAY)

THAT'S INCREDIBLE.

SEPTEMBER 13TH, 2016

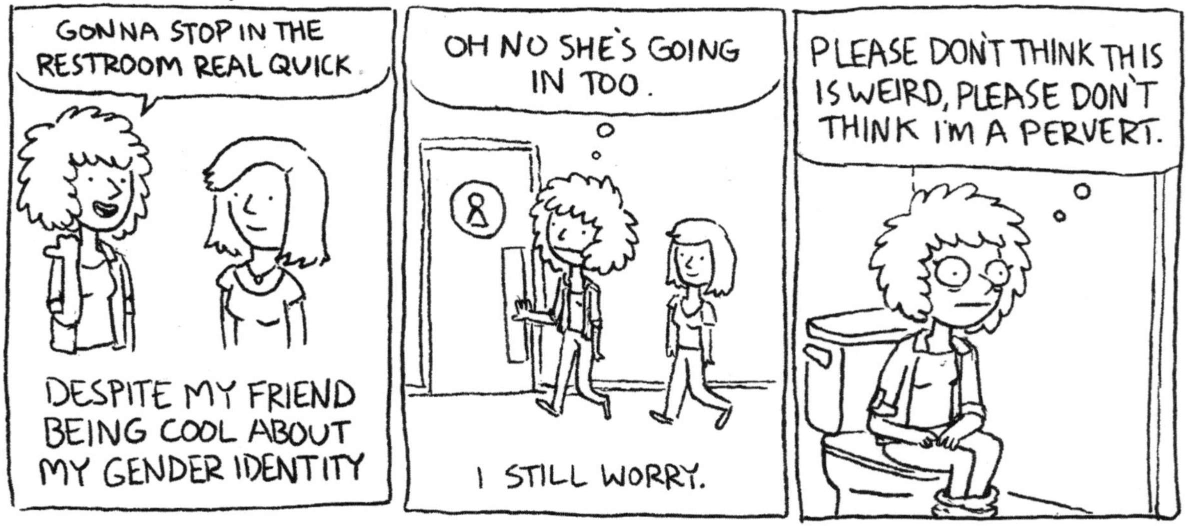
GONNA STOP IN THE RESTROOM REAL QUICK.
DESPITE MY FRIEND BEING COOL ABOUT MY GENDER IDENTITY
OH NO SHE'S GOING IN TOO.
I STILL WORRY.
PLEASE DON'T THINK THIS IS WEIRD, PLEASE DON'T THINK I'M A PERVERT.

SEPTEMBER 14TH, 2016

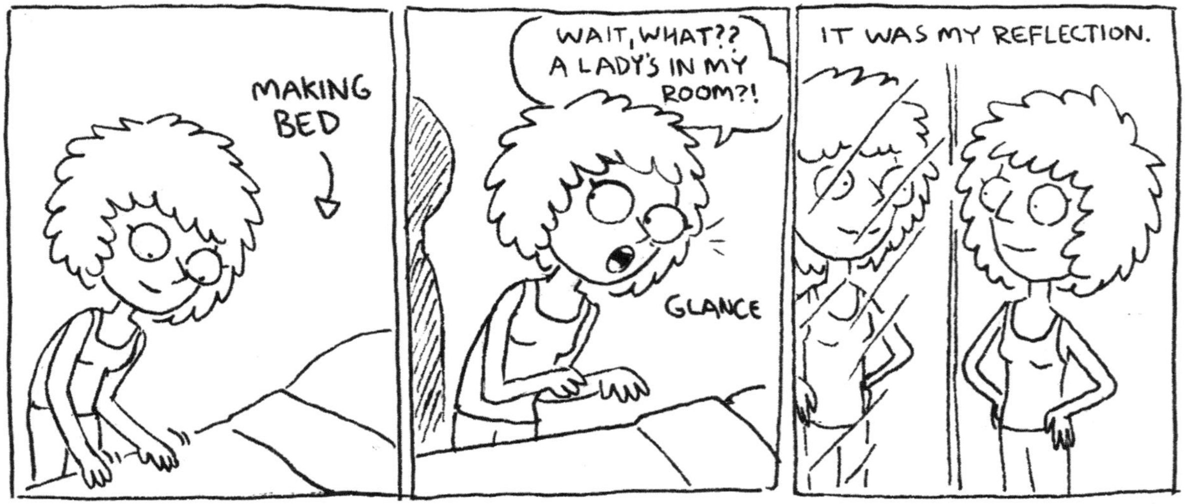
MAKING BED
WAIT, WHAT?? A LADY'S IN MY ROOM?!
GLANCE
IT WAS MY REFLECTION.

SEPTEMBER 15ᵀᴴ, 2016

SPENT THE DAY
WORKING OUT HOW

TO TRANSFER MY
REPRODUCTIVE
MATERIAL TO

WHAT'S THAT?
EVERYTHING I DID
TODAY WAS FOR
NOTHING?
OH, OKAY.

A LONG-TERM
STORAGE FACILITY.

SEPTEMBER 16TH, 2016

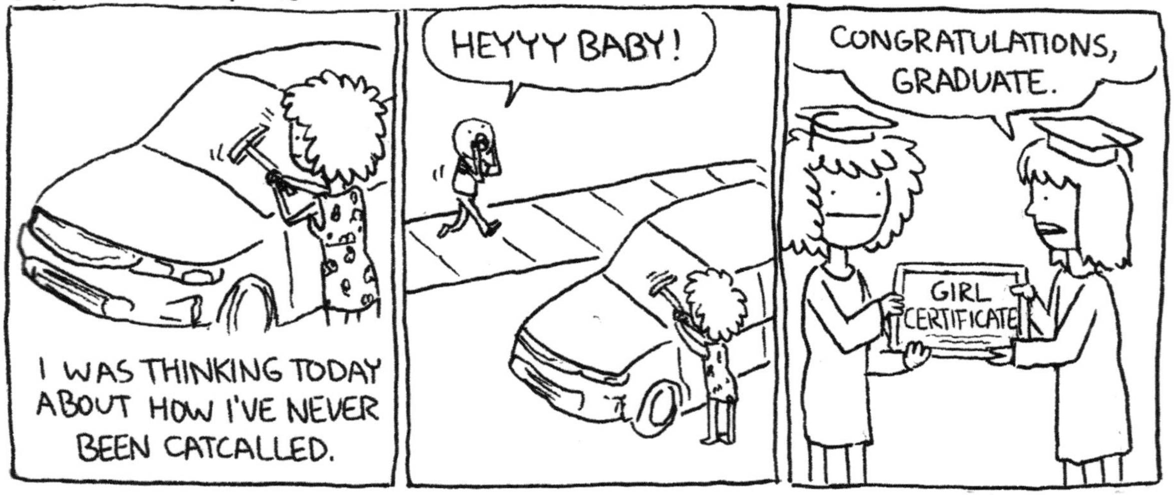
I WAS THINKING TODAY ABOUT HOW I'VE NEVER BEEN CATCALLED.
HEYYY BABY!
CONGRATULATIONS, GRADUATE.
GIRL CERTIFICATE

SEPTEMBER 17TH, 2016

SHAVING MY FACE HAS BEEN GETTING TO ME MORE AND MORE LATELY.

THE EXTRA TIME IN THE MORNING, THE PILING ON CONCEALER TO HIDE THE REMAINING SHADOW..

WORRYING ABOUT IT STILL BEING VISIBLE IN DIRECT SUNLIGHT.. EVERYTHING.

SEPTEMBER 18TH, 2016

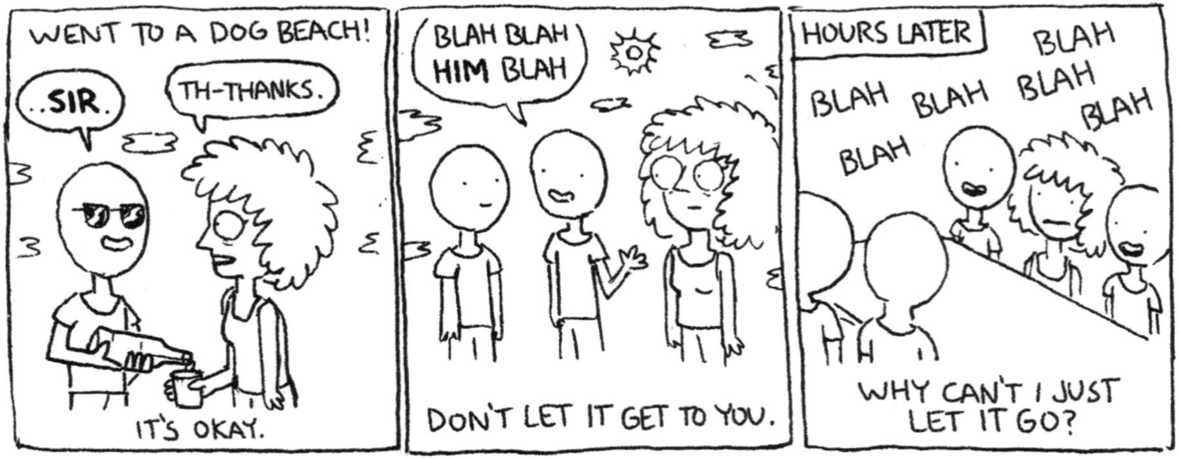
WENT TO A DOG BEACH!
..SIR..
TH-THANKS.
IT'S OKAY.
BLAH BLAH HIM BLAH
DON'T LET IT GET TO YOU.
HOURS LATER
BLAH
BLAH BLAH BLAH
BLAH
BLAH
WHY CAN'T I JUST LET IT GO?

SEPTEMBER 19TH, 2016

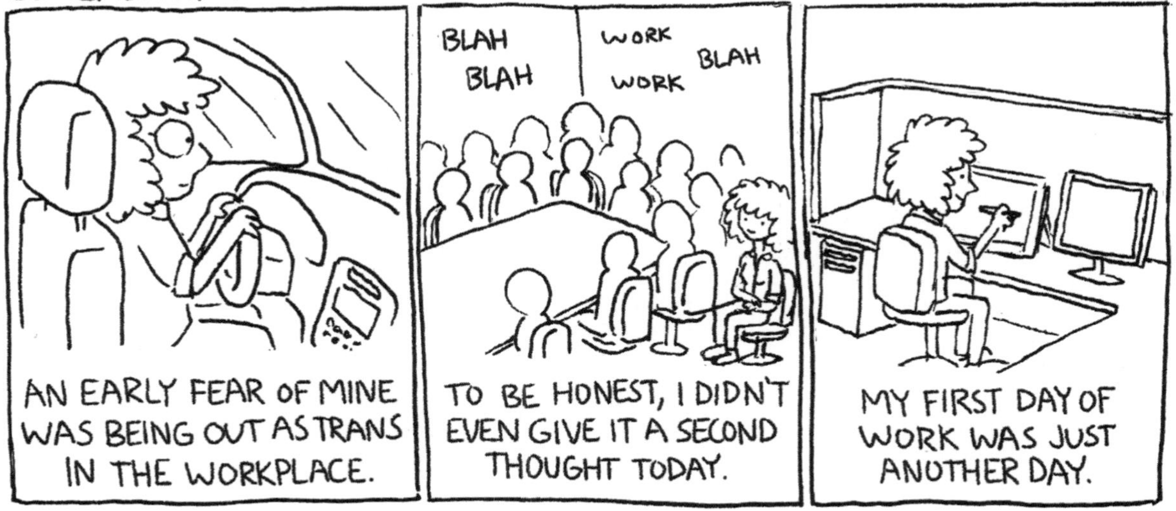

AN EARLY FEAR OF MINE WAS BEING OUT AS TRANS IN THE WORKPLACE.
BLAH BLAH
WORK WORK
BLAH
TO BE HONEST, I DIDN'T EVEN GIVE IT A SECOND THOUGHT TODAY.
MY FIRST DAY OF WORK WAS JUST ANOTHER DAY.

SEPTEMBER 20TH, 2016

SOMETIMES A QUIET VOICE IN THE BACK OF MY MIND SPEAKS UP.

"YOU'LL NEVER BE ANYTHING BUT A FEMINIZED MAN!"

INTERNALIZED TRANSPHOBIA IS AWFUL.

SEPTEMBER 21ST, 2016

I AUTOMATICALLY RAISE THE PITCH OF MY VOICE WHEN ADDRESSING STRANGERS.

I GUESS TO EMPHASIZE MY GENDER IDENTITY.

BUT ALSO I DO WISH MY VOICE WAS NATURALLY HIGHER.

PRE-HORMONES, DAILY BODY HAIR REMOVAL WAS ALL I COULD DO TO HATE MYSELF LESS.

IT'S NOT AS URGENT NOW, BUT I STILL NEED TO GET A COUPLE VISIBLE SPOTS DAILY.

I WONDER HOW MUCH FASTER MY MORNING ROUTINE WOULD BE IF I DIDN'T HAVE TO.

SEPTEMBER 23RD, 2016

G'NIGHT!
HA HA HA HA HA HA HA
..I'M TOO HARD ON MYSELF.

SEPTEMBER 24TH, 2016

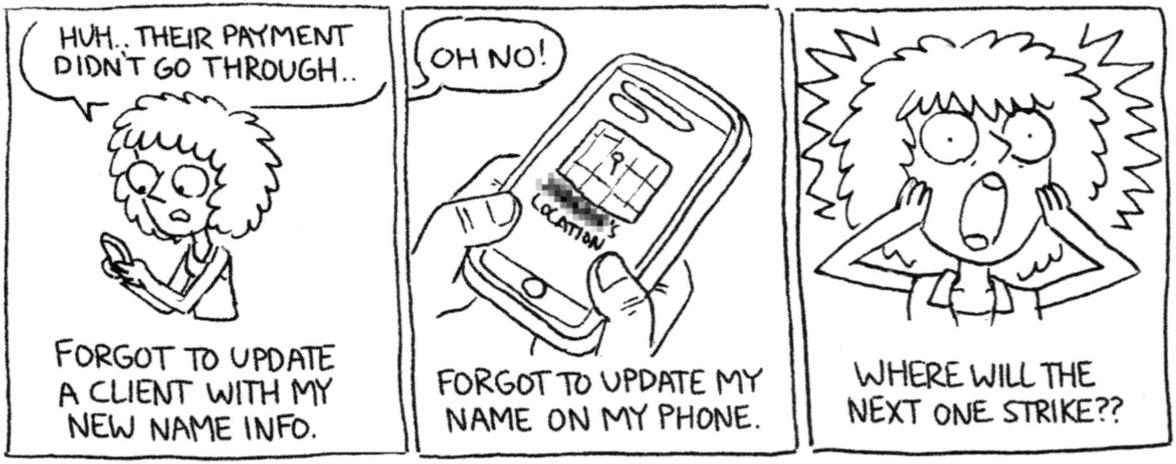
HUH.. THEIR PAYMENT DIDN'T GO THROUGH..
FORGOT TO UPDATE A CLIENT WITH MY NEW NAME INFO.
OH NO!
[redacted]'S LOCATION
FORGOT TO UPDATE MY NAME ON MY PHONE.
WHERE WILL THE NEXT ONE STRIKE??

SEPTEMBER 25TH, 2016

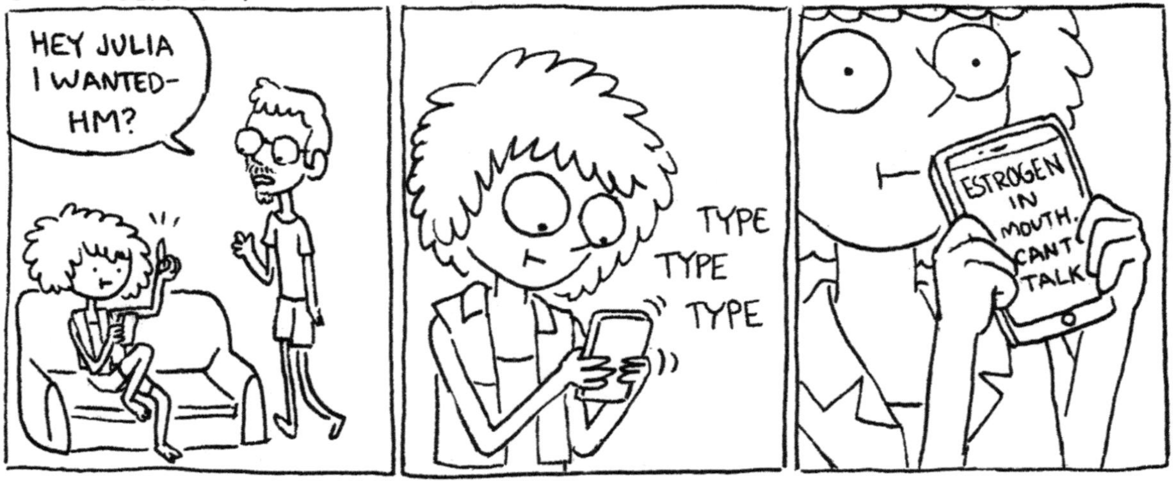

HEY JULIA I WANTED- HM?
TYPE
TYPE
TYPE
ESTROGEN IN MOUTH. CAN'T TALK

SEPTEMBER 26TH, 2016

IT'S ALL WORTH IT FOR THE TIMES I CAN REALLY SEE MYSELF.

IN THOSE MOMENTS, I REALIZE I DON'T FEEL SO DISCONNECTED FROM MYSELF ANYMORE.

I FEEL PRETTY.

I'VE BEEN FEELING PRETTY OKAY LATELY

I'VE BEEN HAVING MORE GOOD DAYS THAN BAD.

SUPER MEAT BOY!!

PROGRESS.

I'M OVER HAVING TO WEAR BRAS DAILY.

IT WAS NEW AND FUN FOR A WHILE BUT—

I'M DONE DONE DONE DONE DONE DONE DONE DONE.

SEPTEMBER 29TH, 2016

I'D ALWAYS HAD A LOT OF SOCIAL ANXIETY, BUT I THOUGHT TRANSITIONING HAD MAYBE HELPED SOME

I WAS WRONG. TURNS OUT I WAS JUST IN A COMFORT ZONE BUBBLE FOR THE PAST YEAR.

I'M SICK OF FEELING PARALYZED AROUND OTHERS. I NEED A NEW THERAPIST.

SEPTEMBER 30ᵀᴴ, 2016

I'M SICK OF TRANSITIONING.

SICK OF PUTTING UP WITH SO MUCH DAILY, SO MUCH MENTAL STRESS.

I DIDN'T ASK FOR THIS.

OCTOBER 1ST, 2016
HERE YOU GO, SIR.
ANOTHER REMINDER.
..THANKS.
UNLESS I WEAR OBVIOUS GENDER SIGNIFIERS I'M READ AS A MAN.
SOB~!
NOT EVEN MY HOME IS SAFE. I DIDN'T NEED THIS TODAY.

IS MY LIFE BETTER FOR TRANSITIONING?

IT'S BEEN ON MY MIND A LOT RECENTLY.

I WANT TO SAY "YES, OF COURSE!" BUT SO OFTEN IT DOESN'T REALLY FEEL LIKE IT.

A LOT OF THE TIME IT FEELS LIKE I SWAPPED OLD BAGGAGE FOR NEW.

OCTOBER 3RD, 2016

I COMPLAIN ABOUT MY BUMPS AND SCRAPES

BUT DESPITE IT ALL I'LL NEVER STOP TAKING MY HORMONES.

I'D NEVER GO BACK.

OCTOBER 4TH, 2016

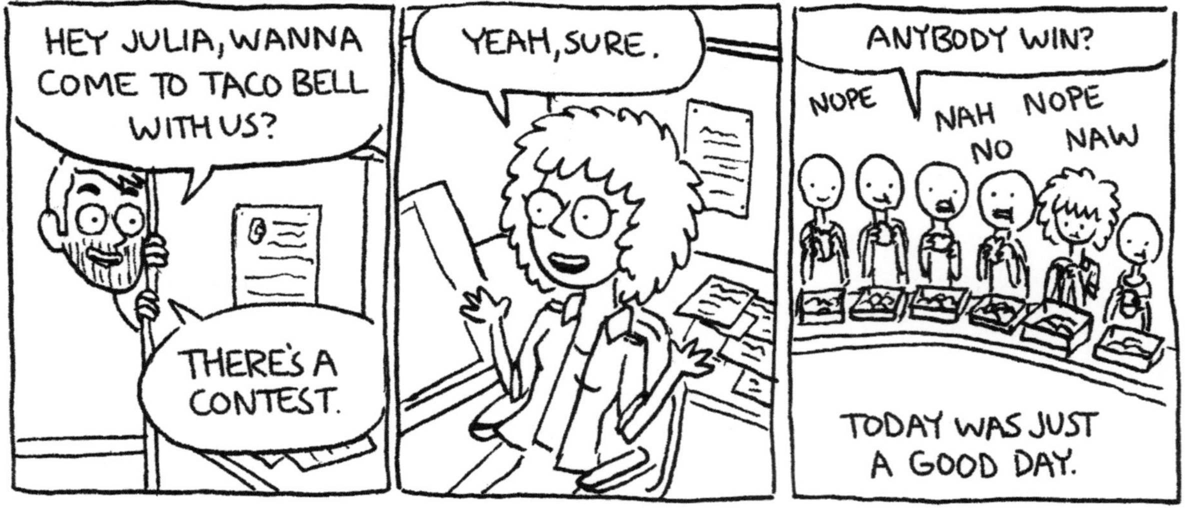

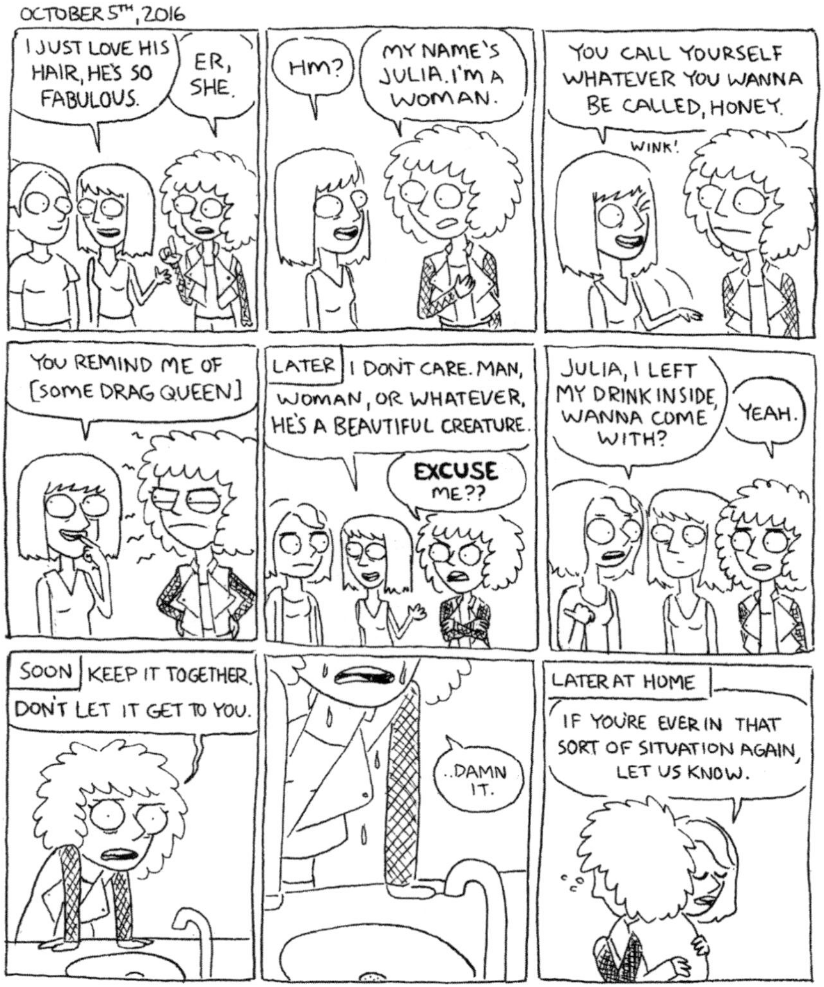
OCTOBER 5TH, 2016
I JUST LOVE HIS HAIR, HE'S SO FABULOUS.
ER, SHE.
HM?
MY NAME'S JULIA. I'M A WOMAN.
YOU CALL YOURSELF WHATEVER YOU WANNA BE CALLED, HONEY.
WINK!
YOU REMIND ME OF [SOME DRAG QUEEN]
LATER
I DON'T CARE. MAN, WOMAN, OR WHATEVER, HE'S A BEAUTIFUL CREATURE.
EXCUSE ME??
JULIA, I LEFT MY DRINK INSIDE, WANNA COME WITH?
YEAH.
SOON
KEEP IT TOGETHER. DON'T LET IT GET TO YOU.
..DAMN IT.
LATER AT HOME
IF YOU'RE EVER IN THAT SORT OF SITUATION AGAIN, LET US KNOW.

OCTOBER 9TH, 2016

IT'S STRANGE SEEING MY
DEPRESSION SO PLAINLY IN
SKETCHBOOKS FROM COLLEGE.

AMIDST IT ALL,

I FOUND DRAWINGS OF
MYSELF AS A WOMAN.

SHUT!

I'D FELT SO EUPHORIC
DRAWING 'EM WITHOUT
UNDERSTANDING WHY.

OCTOBER 10TH, 2016

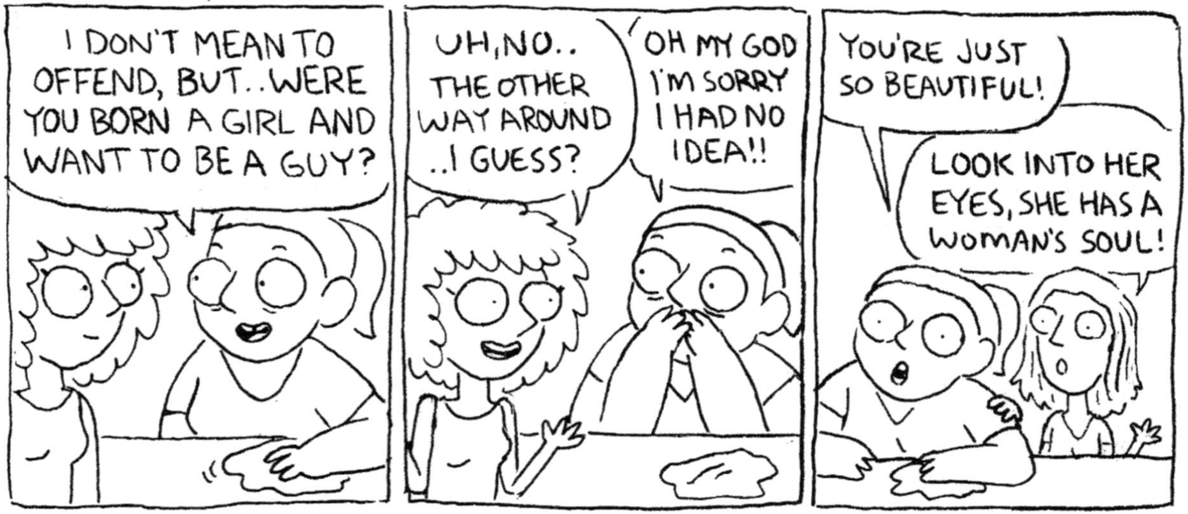
I DON'T MEAN TO OFFEND, BUT.. WERE YOU BORN A GIRL AND WANT TO BE A GUY?
UH, NO.. THE OTHER WAY AROUND ..I GUESS?
OH MY GOD I'M SORRY I HAD NO IDEA!!
YOU'RE JUST SO BEAUTIFUL!
LOOK INTO HER EYES, SHE HAS A WOMAN'S SOUL!

I'VE BEEN FEELING MORE CONFIDENT ABOUT MY LOOKS LATELY.

WHICH HAS LED ME TO DOING MYSELF UP ON THE WEEKEND.

EVEN THOUGH IT'S A LAZY SUNDAY AND I WON'T SEE ANYONE.

I'VE SHOULDERED THE WEIGHT OF SO MANY LIFE CHANGES THIS YEAR.

SO MANY CHANGES.

..I'M UNSTOPPABLE.

OCTOBER 13TH, 2016

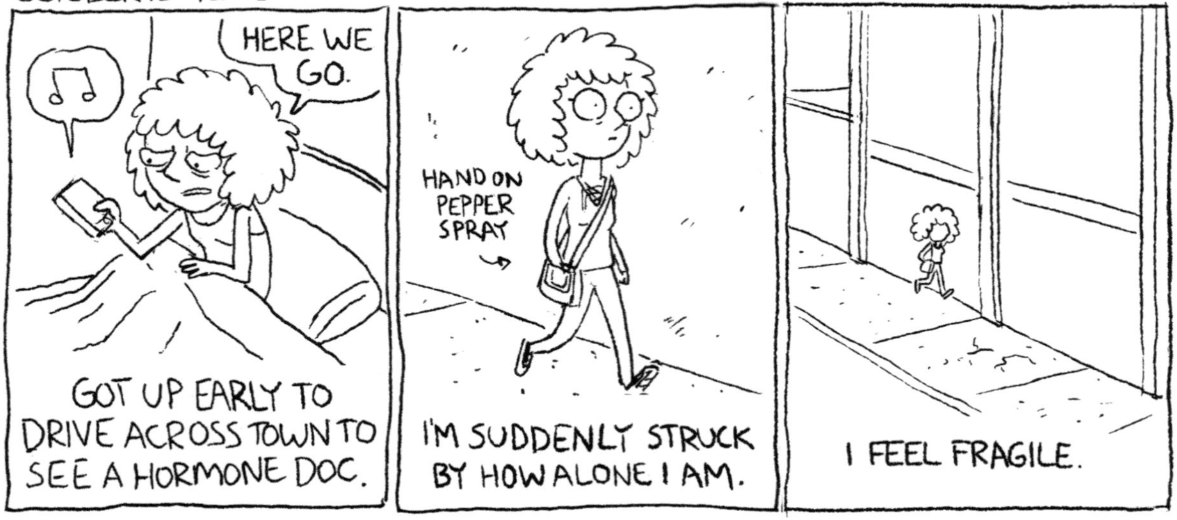
HERE WE GO.
GOT UP EARLY TO DRIVE ACROSS TOWN TO SEE A HORMONE DOC.
HAND ON PEPPER SPRAY
I'M SUDDENLY STRUCK BY HOW ALONE I AM.
I FEEL FRAGILE.

OCTOBER 15TH, 2016

CHILDREN HAVE ALWAYS MADE IT APPARENT I STUCK OUT IN PUBLIC.

RECENTLY I'VE NOTICED THEY NO LONGER STARE IN CONFUSION.

HORMONES ARE WORKING THEIR MAGIC.

OCTOBER 16TH, 2016

THE WORST PART ABOUT NOT HAVING FINISHED FACE LASER:

I CAN NEVER CATCH A BREAK FROM SHAVING EVERY. SINGLE. MORNING.

STOPPING MAKES ME FAR TOO DYSPHORIC.

OCTOBER 17TH, 2016

AS I GET SETTLED INTO LIFE HERE, DATING'S BEEN ON MY MIND.

MY PREVIOUS RELATIONSHIPS HAPPENED SO EFFORTLESSLY.

I WORRY ABOUT MY NEW SMALLER DATING POOL.

I USED TO ENJOY THRIFT SHOPPING. I HAD A PRETTY STANDARD SIZE.

COME ON..

TUG TUG TUG

NOW IT'S HARD ENOUGH TO FIND GOOD-FITTING CLOTHING IN REGULAR STORES.

I GIVE UP.

I REMEMBER WEARING THIS DRESS 5 YEARS AGO. I FELT SO GOOD IN IT.

BUT A GLANCE IN THE MIRROR SHATTERED THE ILLUSION. I WANTED TO BE AS PRETTY AS I FELT.

I FEEL BEAUTIFUL.

OCTOBER 21ST, 2016

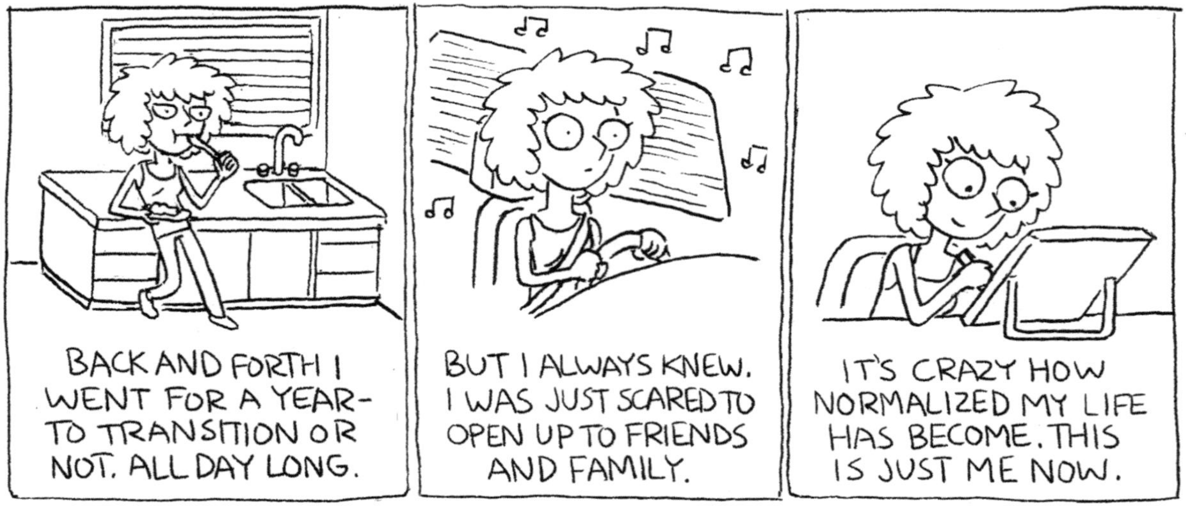
BACK AND FORTH I WENT FOR A YEAR- TO TRANSITION OR NOT. ALL DAY LONG.
BUT I ALWAYS KNEW. I WAS JUST SCARED TO OPEN UP TO FRIENDS AND FAMILY.
IT'S CRAZY HOW NORMALIZED MY LIFE HAS BECOME. THIS IS JUST ME NOW.

OCTOBER 22ND, 2016

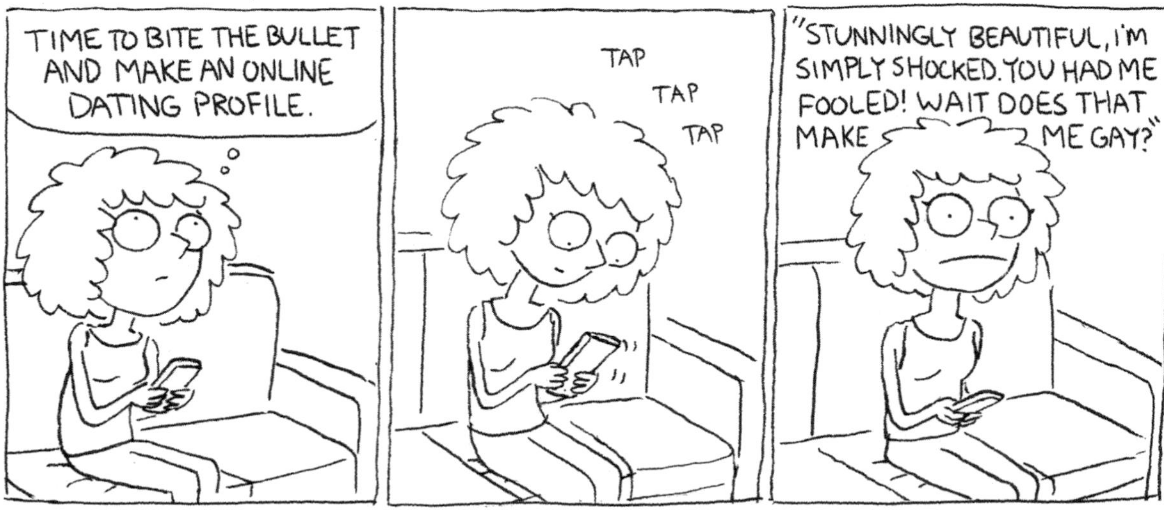
TIME TO BITE THE BULLET AND MAKE AN ONLINE DATING PROFILE.
TAP
TAP
TAP
"STUNNINGLY BEAUTIFUL, I'M SIMPLY SHOCKED. YOU HAD ME FOOLED! WAIT DOES THAT MAKE ME GAY?"

"I WANT YOU INSIDE ME."

"GOOD MORNING GORGEOUS! ..NEVER MIND. TRICKED ONCE AGAIN."

"NO 'WOMEN' WITH A 'THIRD LEG', 'WOMEN' WITH DEEP VOICES, 'WOMEN' WITH A BEARD SHADOW"

THERE HAS TO BE A BETTER WAY.

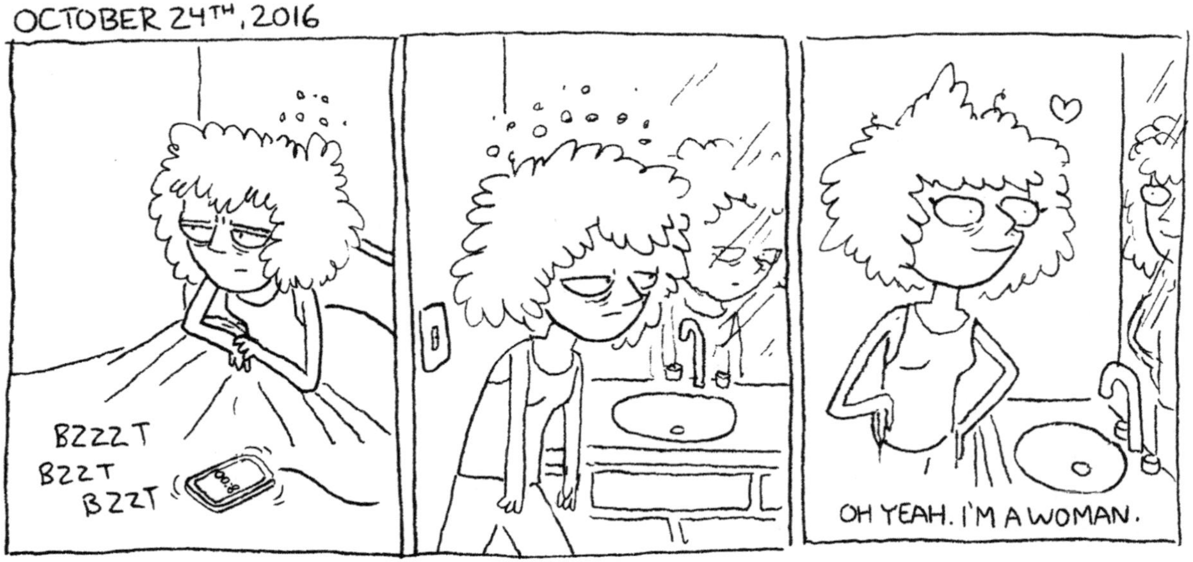
OCTOBER 24TH, 2016
BZZZT
BZZT
BZZT
OH YEAH. I'M A WOMAN.

ONE OF THE MOST WORTHWHILE THINGS I'VE EVER DONE IS BE A VISIBLE TRANS PERSON.

I RECEIVE INCREDIBLE MESSAGES FROM ALL SORTS OF QUEER PEOPLE.

IT HELPS ME FEEL LIKE I'M NOT GOING THROUGH THIS ALONE.

I HAVE A LASER APT ON SATURDAY. FINALLY BACK ON TRACK!!

..BUT AN EVENT CAME UP. I DON'T WANT PEOPLE TO SEE ME WITH POST-LASER STUBBLE.

I GUESS.. I CAN WAIT ANOTHER WEEK TO START IT UP AGAIN.

I TRY NOT TO THINK ABOUT IT TOO MUCH, ALL THE MISSING TIME.

A CHILDHOOD SPENT AS SOMETHING I'M NOT, CONFUSED.

IT CAN BE HARD SOMETIMES THOUGH.

OCTOBER 28TH, 2016

WAIT, YOU'RE TRANS??
I NEVER KNEW YOU WERE TRANS UNITL YOU SAID
YOU'RE GORGEOUS!

GOING BY THE REACTIONS OF STRANGERS, I GUESS I LOOK LESS LIKE A MAN THAN I'D THOUGHT.

Hm.

THE CHANGES HAVE BEEN SO GRADUAL, I DON'T KNOW EXACTLY WHEN IT HAPPENED.

I STILL HAVE TROUBLE SEEING IT, SO I GUESS I JUST HAVE TO TRUST OTHERS FOR NOW.

OCTOBER 29TH, 2016

YEAH, HE
SHE.
I HATE
..HIS-
HERS.
MY
HE'S SO CLOSE!
SHE.
VOICE.

OCTOBER 30TH, 2016

I KNOW I'VE BEEN TOLD
I READ AS A WOMAN.

QUICKLY TURNS AWAY

BUT MAKEUP STILL FEELS
LIKE A PROTECTIVE SHIELD.

ALL THAT'S STOPPING
ME FROM BEING VISUALLY
MISGENDERED.

OCTOBER 31ST, 2016

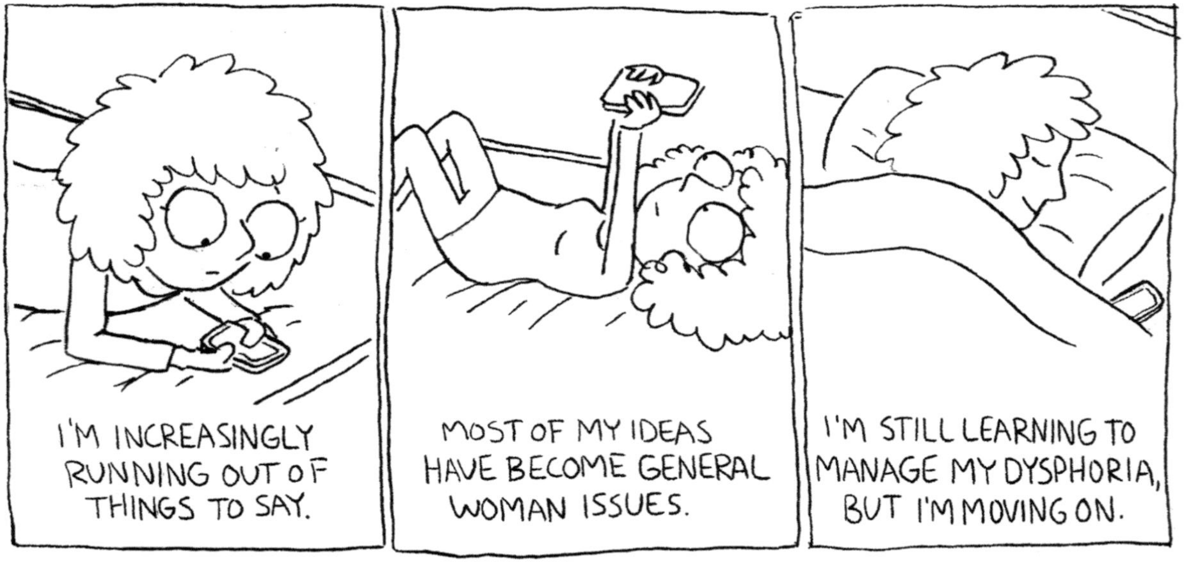
I'M INCREASINGLY RUNNING OUT OF THINGS TO SAY.
MOST OF MY IDEAS HAVE BECOME GENERAL WOMAN ISSUES.
I'M STILL LEARNING TO MANAGE MY DYSPHORIA, BUT I'M MOVING ON.

a letter to my younger self

Hey, friend,

It's been a long time. To be honest, I don't think about you much these days. I try not to, because looking back can be . . . difficult. I try not to dwell, because when I do the tears start welling up, and I find I just can't stop them. You're in so much pain, you don't even know. You've lived with it your whole life and think it's just part of being alive.

It's that underlying discomfort you work so hard to ignore. That almost-tangible feeling of something being wrong. Feeling claustrophobic in a box you can't escape.

Well, it never went away.

I tried my best for so long to shove it down and be the person the world told me to be, but it only intensified as the years went on. I'm not telling you this to scare you; I'm saying it to let you know: It's okay. You're not alone.

There are others like you out there. So many others who feel the same way. If only you knew.

But you have no way of knowing. You don't yet have the vocabulary to be able to describe and understand yourself. You don't have anyone to look to as a point of reference. You have no concept of trans people at all except that of harmful media representation. So you live in a fog of confusion and depression.

And you're going through it alone. Ashamed of yourself. Terrified to ask for help. I wish you knew just how good it feels to let people in. You who can barely function; anxieties ruling your life; so afraid of speaking them aloud for fear of giving them more power.

I know people terrify you. You've been hurt and have every right to have closed yourself off.

I know. I get it.

But, over the years, I've slowly, painstakingly learned they're not all bad. There are people who understand. People who want to lift you up instead of cut you down. Who think your quirks and differences are beautiful rather than things to be ashamed of. And with their help, you get there. You learn how to be yourself, and it's nothing short of incredible. You're incredible.

You're so much stronger than you think you are. You go on to claw your way through hell, a mess of smiles and tears, emerging on the other side a beautiful woman.

I'm sorry you'll have to go through so much turmoil. I'm sorry I didn't realize any of this sooner. You deserve so much better than that. You deserve happiness. I'm sorry. I'm sorry, I'm sorry, I'm sorry.

I love you more than you'll ever know possible, and I'm cheering you on every step of the way. Just please, please hang on. Hang on with everything you've got, because it's worth it. I swear to everything good in this world, it's worth it.

All my love,

Julia

Andrews McMeel Publishing
a division of Andrews McMeel Universal
1130 Walnut Street, Kansas City, Missouri 64106

www.andrewsmcmeel.com

18 19 20 21 22 SDB 10 9 8 7 6 5 4 3 2

ISBN: 978-1-4494-8962-5

Library of Congress Control Number: 2017953229

Editor: Allison Adler
Art Director: Holly Swayne
Production Editor: Elizabeth A. Garcia
Production Manager: Chuck Harper

ATTENTION: SCHOOLS AND BUSINESSES
Andrews McMeel books are available at quantity
discounts with bulk purchase for educational, business, or
sales promotional use. For information, please e-mail the
Andrews McMeel Publishing Special Sales Department:
specialsales@amuniversal.com.